BREATHING LIFE
INTO
THE STONE FORT TREATY

BREATHING LIFE INTO THE STONE FORT TREATY

An Anishinabe Understanding of Treaty One

AIMÉE CRAFT

PURICH
PUBLISHING
LIMITED
SASKATOON, SK. CANADA

Purich Publishing, an imprint of UBC Press
2029 West Mall; Vancouver, BC; Canada; V6T 1Z2
www.ubcpress.ca
26 25 24 23 22 21 20 19 18   6 5 4 3 2

Library and Archives Canada Cataloguing in Publication

Craft, Aimée, 1980-
    breathing life into the Stone Fort Treaty : an Anishinabe understanding of Treaty One / Aimée Craft.

    Includes bibliographical references and index.
    ISBN 978-1-895830-64-4

    1. Canada. Treaties, etc. 1871 Aug. 3. 2. Ojibwa Indians — Manitoba — Treaties. 3. Ojibwa Indians — Legal status, laws, etc. — Manitoba. 4. Ojibwa Indians — Canada — Government relations. I. Title.

KE7749.O45C73 2013   346.7104›320899733307127   C2012-908315-1
KF5662.O45C73 2013

Edited, designed, and typeset by Donald Ward.
Cover painting: Bi-go-ima nemi — She Dances Anywhere, by Linus Woods.
Cover design by Jamie Olson.
Index by Ursula Acton.

Printed and bound in Canada.

Canadä

UBC Press gratefully acknowledges the financial support for our publishing program of the Government of Canada (through the Canada Book Fund), the Canada Council for the Arts, and the British Columbia Arts Council.
Ais book is printed on 100 per cent post-consumer, recycled, and ancient-forest-friendly paper.

Contents

Part Three: Anishinabe Inaakonigewin

Part Four: Living the Treaty

Acknowledgments

After almost a decade of working in Canadian Aboriginal law, I took the opportunity to follow another path and to explore Treaty One from an Indigenous legal perspective. This book is a revision of my thesis prepared in the context of a Law and Society Graduate program at the University of Victoria. I am grateful for all the guidance and mentorship that was offered, from my supervisory committee; Jeremy Webber and Michael Asch, professors; John Borrows, Judy Fudge, Michael M'Gonigle, Jean Friesen, Heidi Stark, and Taiaiake Alfred, my readers and editors; Kerry Sloan and Jeanette Gevikoglu, and Megan Menzies. I am also grateful to the University of Victoria, the Law Foundation of British Columbia, Legal Aid Manitoba, and Indigenous Peoples and Governance (IPG) for their support. My Elders Ron, Greg, Aldeen, Dave, Gerald, Joe, Peter, and Sherry reminded me throughout the process that we are all connected. They kept me centred, focused and helped me grow as a person, as a thinker and in my own spirit. It was an amazing experience. What I have to show for it is because of them, but, of course, the mistakes are my own.

Miigwech to my family, my friends, my relatives — in Victoria, in Manitoba and all over Turtle Island — you have inspired me.

Miigwech to my Mom and Dad. You give so much and ask for so little.

Miigwech to my *mishomis*. You taught me all that I needed to know to be *Anishinabe*, a good person. You showed me that love and kindness really have no limits.

Miigwech to my ancestors. May you know that I carry your thoughts for us in my little heart.

Miigwech Kije-Manitou.

Dedication

For all of those who have gone on, those who are here today, and in particular, to those who are yet to come. May you honour the treaty relationship.

Author's Note: The Anishinabe (Ojibway, Chipewa, Ojibwe or Anishinaabe) language, *anishinabemowin*, has many dialects. In some areas, Anishinabe people will refer to the plural form as Anishinabek or Anishinabeg. Some will also use a double vowel, e.g. Anishinaabeg, to refer to the long sound of that vowel.

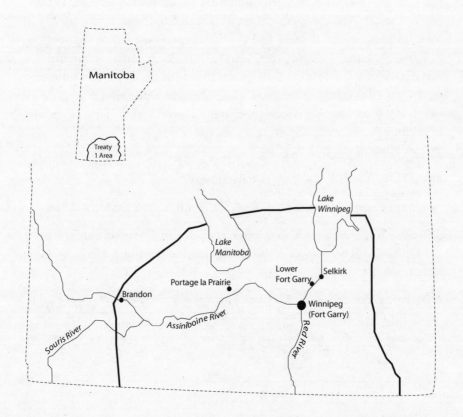

Lower Fort Garry (the Stone Fort) was built in 1830 by the Hudson's Bay Company on the western bank of the Red River, 20 miles north of the original Fort Garry, which is now in Winnipeg. Treaty 1 was signed there.

Foreword

I first met Aimée when she travelled to the west coast to further her understanding of Indigenous law. As an accomplished lawyer, she brought a rich knowledge of the role of Canadian law in structuring foundational relationships. Her expertise in issues related to Indigenous land rights, resources, consultation, human rights, and governance was readily apparent to everyone she met. What distinguished Aimée, however, was a special attentiveness to the constructive role which language and tradition can play in legal affairs. Thus, when she came to Vancouver Island, she immediately sought out Elders and other Indigenous knowledge keepers to learn more about the development and transmission of law within this context. As a result, she quickly deepened her insights about the role of traditional law in Salish life, and this redoubled her determination to research and write about the laws and teachings of her Anishinaabe Elders living in Manitoba, Ontario, and beyond. The book you now hold in your hands is the culmination of this work. Aimée's careful research and clear writing presents a vision of law which places treaties and Indigenous traditions at the heart of Canada's law.

When First Nations peoples made treaties with the Crown, they deployed powers of reason, persuasion, and judgement. Their active participation made a difference to the process by which treaties were negotiated and the terms they eventually contained. In taking a significant role in their development, First Nations inevitably weighed and balanced their perceptions of the Crown's views and, in light of the information available, they made decisions about the Crown's words and deeds. This is all to say that First Nations had their own ideas about what treaties meant for their way of life and their future. In fact, many influences would have informed First Nations' evaluations of these matters. Indigenous perceptions of economics, sociology, politics, spirituality, and the power of personality would have all played an important part in deciding how to analyze the government's words. Intermixed with these forces was the role of Indigenous law. Though differently expressed across diverse societies, law sets standards for judgement which assist communities in considering how to receive and deal with peoples and nations from other lands. Thus, it should come as no surprise that Indigenous law helped First Nations make judgements regarding how they should relate to people representing the British Crown. Indigenous law was not only present during the debate, deliberation, and discussion leading up to and during treaty negotiations, Indigenous law also played a significant role in the development of conditions which First Nations negotiated as part of these agreements.

This book shows the immense power of Indigenous law in the treaty-making enterprise. Using a clear and straightforward style, Aimée examines the role of Anishinaabe law in the creation of Treaty One, in what is now southern Manitoba. She does a masterful job of weaving an Anishinaabe context throughout this work as she demonstrates how knowledge of Indigenous law makes a considerable difference in understanding the nature and scope of treaty agreements. While Aimée would be the first to admit that any academic discussion of Anishinaabe law during Treaty One's negotiation only reveals the tip of this iceberg, she nevertheless provides important informational keys which help to unlock basic Anishinaabe concepts vital to comprehending its meaning. This has led her to produce an exceptional work of great insight and consequence. This book holds significant potential for shifting our views about the basic nature of law in structuring, interpreting, and sustaining Crown-Indigenous relationships, not only in Treaty One lands, but throughout Canada. It is a must read for everyone interested in understanding the importance of Indigenous law in Canada.

John Borrows, JD, PhD, FRSC
Robina Professor in Law, Policy & Society
University of Minnesota Law School

Treaty Interpretation and Implementation:
Entwined Disconnection

Only thus can hope be bright that there might come a tomorrow when you, the descendants of the settlers of our lands, can say to the world, "Look, we came and were welcomed, and then we wrought much despair; but we are also men of honour and integrity and we set to work in cooperation, we listened and we learned, we gave our support, and today we live in harmony with the first peoples of this land who now call us brothers." We hope that tomorrow will come.

Dave Courchene, Sr.
Grand Chief of Manitoba[1]

Overview

Treaties are solemn agreements between people. In order to interpret and implement a treaty, we look to its spirit and intent, and consider what was contemplated by the parties at the time the treaty was negotiated. Both parties' understandings of the treaty need to be taken into account in its interpretation and implementation.

In seeking understandings, we cannot assume that the parties shared their views of the treaty or that they came to a "common understanding" of it. Even if a "common understanding" existed, it may have been limited to an agreement to share the land, and it may have been that each party had a different understanding of what sharing the land actually entailed.

To understand what was negotiated at the time of treaty, and to construct what it should mean today, requires an independent understanding of each perspective, which includes an understanding of the normative values and laws of the Indigenous[2] parties. In the context of the numbered treaties, and in particular Treaty One, one must remember that the agreements were made in a particular social, political, cultural, and legal context that was not one-sided. To understand the numbered treaties, we need to understand them as part of an evolving tradition of treaty-making with a long history. At Treaty One, Anishinabe procedural laws helped secure the negotiations and opened the door to a "gathering of spirit."[3] In addition to procedural norms, substantive Anishinabe legal principles formed part of the Anishinabe understanding of Treaty One.

Today, Indigenous interpretations of treaties are needed, so that we can continue to breathe life into what are essentially relationship documents, while accepting that past interpretations have resulted in significant disagreement. Understanding the treaty requires depth, consideration, and knowledge. To understand the treaty is to know more than the written text. While it is not possible to go back in time to relive the negotiations, there is benefit in understanding how and why the parties negotiated, even if the full substance of that agreement cannot be discovered. It may be that there was no meeting of minds or common intention at the time of Treaty One, beyond the agreement to share the land in a spirit of peace and coexistence, and that we are now faced with elaborating an appropriate meaning of a treaty that both parties considered they had made.[4]

In a submission to the *Royal Commission on Aboriginal Peoples* in 1992, Peter Atkinson suggested solutions could be found by trying to understand our views:

> If you are looking for solutions, that is where we should start. We should start trying to understand each other. Our people have done a lot in trying to understand your people. Now I think it is time that they try to understand us, listen to us, listen to what we want, what we need.[5]

The themes taken up in this book allow us to consider how we can support a better interpretation of treaty by looking to the Anishinabe understanding of the treaty they made with the Crown, rooted as it was in procedural and substantive norms derived from Anishinabe *inaakonigewin* (law). Those norms and legal principles shaped the Anishinabe position in ways that were manifest in the treaty negotiations themselves.

Drawing on practices of treaty making prior to Treaty One, it is clear that in 1871 the parties relied extensively on Anishinabe protocols and procedural laws in the context of the Treaty One negotiations. In addition, kinship relationships, the obligations derived from them, and a sense of the sacred obligations involved in treaty making informed the agreement that was made between the parties. In particular, the kinship between a mother and child was invoked by the parties; the Crown negotiators relying on it primarily to secure good terms with the Anishinabe and the Anishinabe advocating for a commitment to ensuring a good life while respecting and preserving their autonomy.

By considering Treaty One from the perspective of the Anishinabe, especially Anishinabe laws, or *inaakonigewin,* and normative expectations, one can obtain a better understanding of why there are discrepancies in interpretations of the treaty. Exploring the historical record of the negotiations and the oral history surrounding the treaty negotiations help draw out the differing and sometimes competing understandings of the treaty, many of which continue to this day, in particular, in relation to the effect of the treaty on legal relationships to land. They help illuminate questions about the interpretation of the treaty, including what would be necessary in order to implement it in accordance with its signatories' understandings. This perspective has, to date, been generally disregarded by the Crown and the courts, and has remained relatively uncanvassed in academia (with the exception of some anthropological oral historical projects and the work of some scholars).[6]

In order to interpret and implement treaties as meaningful agreements, the different and differing understandings need to be addressed. Although the treaty parties may have understood that they each had differing perspectives, each was guided by its own understandings, including its own legal tradition and jurisdiction. While the task of implementation may prove challenging, it is a challenge that is firmly rooted in our history, given that many of us have lived in a way that has given meaning to treaties, despite disagreement. I do not propose to address the issues relating to the implementation of treaties in this book, but rather suggest that the key to achieving implementation is to begin with an understanding of different views about the meaning of treaty. In the following chapters, we see that if Anishinabe legal principles are set aside, especially in relation to land and treaty making, we cannot give effect to the spirit and intent of treaty.

Courts: Treaty Interpretation and Implementation

One might wonder why, to date, the treaties have not been given full effect. The short answer is that treaty interpretation has been largely dependent on federal policy and Canadian common law courts. The courts have developed a set of interpretive rules, specific to treaty interpretation, that are largely modelled on statutory canons of construction. Generally, interpretation is structured around the principle of large, liberal, and generous interpretation, with ambiguities being resolved in favour of Aboriginal people.

The Supreme Court of Canada finds that "treaties are a solemn exchange of promises made by the Crown and various First Nations,"[7] and that "the words in the treaty must not be interpreted in their strict technical sense nor subjected to rigid modern rules of construction."[8] Treaties are to be understood as they would have been construed by the Aboriginal signatories, and interpreted flexibly, with the use of extrinsic evidence: "If there is evidence by conduct or otherwise as to how the parties understood the terms of the treaty, then such understanding and practice is of assistance in giving content to the term or terms."[9]

Yet the application of treaty interpretation principles by Canadian courts has not resulted in a meaningful or complete understanding of Aboriginal-Crown treaties, nor has it achieved the court's goal of remedying disadvantage.[10] Indigenous principles of treaty interpretation rarely find their way into the Canadian courts. Consideration of Indigenous laws that made treaties are generally absent from the legal analysis. In many cases, treaty interpretation has favoured the perspective of the Crown and largely set aside Indigenous perspectives. In practice, many court decisions have resulted in narrow understandings of treaties, often limiting the treaty rights in space and in time. Why is it that the current elaboration of that foundational intention rests primarily in the Crown's understanding of treaty? Why is the Anishinabe oral version of the treaty systematically discounted in practice by courts and the Crown? Should only one of the systems of law that were relied on for the negotiations of the treaty form the framework of interpretation?[11] Or should Anishinabe legal principles, both procedural and substantive, inform the interpretation and implementation of treaties today?

How can years of uni-directional understanding, based on a written text and privileging the Crown's view, be reconsidered in order to give voice to the Anishinabe understanding of treaty? In dissent in the Horseman case, Wilson J. was intent on looking at the historical context in which the treaties were signed to understand what the treaties meant for the parties:

> These treaties were the product of negotiation between very different cultures and the language used in them probably does not reflect, and should not be expected to reflect, with total accuracy each party's understanding of their effect at the time they were entered into. This is why the courts must be especially sensitive to the broader historical context in which such treaties were negotiated. They must be prepared to look at that historical context in order to ensure that they reach a proper understanding of the meaning that particular treaties held for their signatories at the time.[12]

Following the enactment of the *Constitution Act, 1982*,[13] a body of literature emerged that is somewhat critical of Canadian constitutional Aboriginal law, and skeptical of how constitutional legal protection of treaty and Aboriginal rights are to be given "legal" effect.[14] We must remember that treaties are agreements between two parties in which neither party's perspective should be privileged. Is it fair that one of the parties to the treaty carries the authority of interpretation?[15] Sidney Harring finds that the "Indians" had their own reasons and agendas that informed the negotiations, some of which were legal in nature.[16] There is an expanding view that Indigenous legal tradition should be given weight, not only by reason of common law acceptance but because it has its own inherent purpose and value.[17]

Indigenous Treaty Iterpretation

Some Indigenous scholars and practitioners have approached treaty interpretation from an Indigenous legal perspective.[18] For example, Robert Williams Jr., in his work *Linking Arms Together*, refers to treaties as a vision of law and peace within a burgeoning system of intercultural diplomacy.[19] Harold Johnson explains in *Two Families* that Indigenous people viewed the treaty as an agreement to adopt settlers and to enter into a kinship relationship with them, defined primarily by an obligation to *share* in the bounty of Mother Earth. Johnson also suggests that the sharing relationship, forged between the treaty "families" and the Creator, is a covenant[20] that cannot be breached and cannot be voided, regardless of action or inaction.[21] Heidi Kiiwetinepinesiik Stark explains the treaty relationship among nations in terms of respect, responsibility, and renewal.[22]

My approach to research relating to Anishinabe law and treaties starts from the premise that Anishinabe law is all about relationships:[23] relationships among and between ourselves, relationships with other animate beings. These relationships give rise to rights, obligations, and responsibilities. Rights, obligations, and responsibilities are exercised both individually and collectively by the Anishinabe.

To begin to understand the Anishinabe perspective, I have chosen to triangulate between the written record, oral histories, and Indigenous knowledge. Using the written accounts of the commissioners' speeches, the written summaries of the proceedings recorded by third parties, treaty-era correspondence from chiefs to Crown officials, historical newspaper accounts, minutes of pre- and post-treaty meetings, and recorded oral history gives us an impression of what was being negotiated at the time of treaty.[24]

This book explores five distinct concepts that support this interpretation. First, prior to negotiating Treaty One, Anishinabe practices of treaty making with Indigenous nations, fur traders, and the British Crown resulted in each treaty partner adopting, to some extent, Anishinabe legal principles as foundations of treaty practices and relationships, setting an important precedent for the recognition of Indigenous ways of making treaty. Second, the particular context of the Treaty One negotiations, including settler expansion into the west, the sale of land from the Hudson's Bay Company to Canada, and the creation of the province of Manitoba in 1870 placed pressure on both the Crown and the Anishinabe to enter into treaty. Third, the reliance on and use of Anishinabe protocols in the negotiations illustrates the use of Anishinabe procedural laws in the Treaty One negotiations, and informs the substantive expectations of the treaty, including the sacredness of the treaty. Fourth, while each party negotiated the relationship on the basis of kinship and referred to the Queen as mother, the Anishinabe kinship norms invoked duties of love, care, kindness, equal treatment of all children, and the overarching obligation of a mother to ensure a good life for her children. Finally, the Anishinabe understandings of their relationship to Mother Earth informed what could be negotiated in terms of sharing the land with the incoming settlers. All these concepts lead to the understanding that Treaty One was an agreement to share in the land, for the purposes of agriculture, in a spirit of "peace and good will" with assurances of an "allowance they are to count upon and receive year by year from Her Majesty's bounty and benevolence."[25] Even the words of the treaty text reflect these understandings, which were, unfortunately, understood substantively, or at least put into action very differently by the Anishinabe and the Crown.

The Anishinabe generally think of the impacts of their actions in terms of future generations, often seven generations ahead. The Treaty One relationship began 140 years ago — or seven generations ago. Is the treaty relationship we are living today that which our ancestors would have envisioned for us? What follows is an attempt to help better understand what they might have consented to on our behalf, based on their system of law and norms.

Part 1

What Came Before Treaty One

Skilled Negotiators and Diplomats: The Anishinabe and Indigenous, Fur Trade, and Crown Treaties

The Anishinabe were skilled negotiators and treaty makers. In their negotiations, they employed Anishinabe laws and normative principles. Their political, military, and trade alliances among themselves and with other Indigenous nations gave them extensive experience in treaty and alliance building, modelled on Indigenous legal traditions. Their extensive history of negotiations and making of "trade treaties"[1] or "commercial compacts"[2] with fur traders established the mutually respectful relationships in which the fur traders moulded themselves to Anishinabe ways and expectations. In addition, the Anishinabe had a history of treaty making with the British Crown; this included the Anishinabe further east and those to the south, in the United States, with whom the Anishinabe of the Treaty One area were linked by kin and clan.

The combined political, geographical, and historical context led to the particular circumstances that allowed the early numbered treaties to be negotiated. Each party brought specific understandings and normative expectations into the treaty negotiations, and emerged days later with agreements based on and perceived in their own ways of understanding. In attempting to understand the treaties, some have hypothesized that the Indians were taken advantage of, that they did not understand the terms of land surrender and sale, and that they could not read or comprehend complex legal terminology.[3] Others point to the difficulties encountered with translation, both in the quality and in the conceptual impossibility of translating certain terms. In *The Birth of Western Canada*, Stanley wrote that "[t]he Natives seldom understood the terms of the contract. The disparity in power and interests between the signatories reduced the treaties to mere grants of such terms as the weaker people might accept without active resistance. . . ."[4]

More nuanced perspectives have been drawn out in part by scholars such as D. J. Hall, Jean Friesen, Arthur Ray, J. R. Miller, and Frank Tough. Hall wrote in 1984 that the "treaty-making process of the 1870s is undergoing reassessment."[5] Hall acknowledged that "[m]any researchers . . . have begun to look at the evidence from an Indian perspective; they have contended that the Indians played a much larger role in shaping the treaties than had been admitted in the earlier works."[6] Hall posed some foundational and important questions in relation to the negotiations and the treaty:

> Why did the Indians sign such a limited document after the lengthy struggle to gain more extensive concessions? Were they merely rely-ing on verbal or "outside" promises to be as binding as those written down? Certainly to the Indians, such promises were binding, and that would probably account in part for what happened. But they were not quite so naïve about the ways of the white man as to trust ver-bal promises entirely. In all likelihood, the Commissioner at the time explained that the provisions included in the treaty were in line with those of previous treaties; or close enough so as not to mark a major departure; after all, he had already slightly exceeded his instructions. Other promises would not be forgotten by the government.[7]

Subsequently, academics such as Jean Friesen have argued that Indian leaders made the best deals they could in exchange for the surrender of their lands, given the difficult situations they were faced with. Friesen ar-gues that the negotiations were highly informed by the past relationships between the Anishinabe and the Hudson's Bay Company (HBC), as well as by the Anishinabe need to ensure their future economic security. Fri-esen concludes that the Anishinabe understood the treaty as a surrender of land, and that by making "the best deal they could," they protected their control over the natural resources and their way of life.[8] In her view, there is some truth to the imbalance of power and implicit or explicit threat that the land would be taken anyway, but "to portray the Indian leaders as weak tools of the treaty commissioners is very misleading."[9]

To a certain extent, the relationship with the HBC and the adherence to the protocols are responsible for the incomplete understandings of treaty

that have resulted. In part, the misunderstandings were attributable to differing values and legal principles that informed the views of each party. I
share Friesen and Miller's views that security and reciprocity of relationships were the underlying motives that led to the making of the western
treaties. I also agree with Friesen that the Crown negotiators for Treaty
One did not understand the significance of the social contract that was
being brokered by the Anishinabe. The negotiators viewed the treaties as
finalizing, once and for all, the clearing of title while, for the Anishinabe, it
was "the beginning of a continuing relation of mutual obligation."[10] Friesen
also argues that we should take into account the political and economic
perceptions of the Anishinabe at the time the treaties were made, and that
new perspectives on treaties should look to the politics and approach of
Indians to others (fictive kinship)[11] and the adaptation of fur trade politics
(or trade treaties).[12] Bruce White refers to the use of kinship language in
the fur trade and how this affected the words that infused the Treaty negotiations and solidified the relationship between "The Great Mother," the
Queen, and "her Children." In particular, White notes that "[t]he power
and extent of these new relationships were based on the degree in which
they could be made to resemble the social and economic relations that existed among family members."[13]

Ray, Miller, and Tough, like Friesen, look at the treaty records to dem-
onstrate how the Indians were concerned with securing their livelihood.
"Because they had an economic and social agenda for securing a future
livelihood, the details of the terms of the treaties had to be negotiated. Otherwise an agreement would not have been reached."[14] Sidney Harring takes
a slightly different view, relating his argument to something akin to shared
land use, rather than retained rights over resources. Harring equates the
surrender clause in the treaty to cessions of some land use rights, but not
to a full surrender of land.[15] In *Bounty and Benevolence*, Ray, Miller, and
Tough conclude that the understanding of the numbered treaties should
be broadened:

> beyond the narrow legal terminology contained in the official treaty
> texts. Aboriginal title was not explained, the significance of reserves
> was blurred by assuring Indians of an ongoing access to lands not
> taken up, and concerns about land needs and livelihood were placat-
> ed by invoking the Queen's good intentions.... [T]he written version
> of these treaties was not complete.[16]

The general consensus among these scholars in post-colonial legal history is that looking at the written text of a treaty does not do justice to the complexity of the issues and interactions that exist. I agree with those who go on to say that the social and political contexts, including the Indigenous forms of normative ordering, must be taken into account.[17]

Many factors contributed to the making of the treaty with the First Nations who lived in the area of Treaty One, which is today referred to as southern Manitoba. The collision of the Anishinabe experience with the HBC for over a century and a half, the recent influx of White settlers, the Red River Resistance, as well as the need to secure a future for children and grandchildren, resulted in particular circumstances that allowed for the making of a treaty of alliance between the Anishinabe and the Queen. Contextual factors informed the negotiation of Treaty One, or "set the table" for the agreement between the Crown and the Anishinabe. Although I will canvass only briefly the various factors that induced the Anishinabe to enter into treaty, they remain an important sub-text for understanding the negotiations. First, I will consider the longstanding diplomatic relationships between the Anishinabe and other Indigenous groups from surrounding territories to be the pillars of Anishinabe diplomacy and treaty making. Second, I will canvass the impact of generations of interactions with fur traders and the culture of trade treaties, as traders adopted Anishinabe ways in order to conclude economic agreements. Third, I will explore the approach to treaty making between the Anishinabe and the Crown, over the century preceding Treaty One, as an important precedential relationship-building exercise that was conducted in accordance with Anishinabe legal principles.

Indigenous Treaties

Prior to the arrival of Europeans on Turtle Island,[18] the Anishinabe had longstanding diplomatic relationships among the different groups (or tribes) within their nation,[19] as well as with other Indigenous peoples. These relationships persist to this day, and are the foundational indicators of Anishinabe diplomacy; they illustrate Indigenous principles of normative ordering that were applied to the making of the peace treaties. "These 'treaty processes' were grounded in the worldviews, language, knowledge systems, and political cultures of the nations involved, and they were governed by the common Indigenous ethics of justice, peace, respect, reciprocity, and accountability."[20]

The Council of Three Fires[21] was the historic system of alliance developed among the Anishinabe (Ojibway, Odawa, and Potawatomi nations), through which governance was conducted via public meetings aimed at union, alliance, treaty making, and renewal:

> [E]ach band or community has its own chiefs, and manages its own affairs, within the limits of its territory, quite independently of other tribes of the same nation; but in matters which affect the whole nation, a general council is called, composed of all or a majority of the chiefs of the different tribes.[22]

This confederacy maintained alliances and relations with the other nations that shared or bordered their territories, such as the Iroquois (Haudenosaunee) in the east, and the Sioux (Dakota) in the west. The primary aim of those relationships was peace, often associated with the resolution of territorial disputes: they recognized each nation's independence, nationhood, and sovereignty. "Both political entities assumed that they would share the territory, that they would both take care of their shared hunting grounds, and that they would remain separate, sovereign, self-determining, and independent nations."[23]

The relationships of peace between the Anishinabe and their neighbouring nations to the east and west were essential for their sustenance and survival. Often, war was the catalyst for alliance and treaty.[24] The concept of Indigenous political diplomacy existed long before the arrival of Europeans, and was widespread among tribes.[25] Peace and friendship was brokered between the Anishinabe and the Haudenosaunee as early as 1701, and regularly reaffirmed:

> The agreement was orally transacted and is recorded on a wampum belt (a memory device with shells forming pictures, sewn onto strings of animal hide and bound together). The 1701 belt has an image of a "bowl with one spoon." It refers to the fact that both Nations would share their hunting grounds in order to obtain food. The single wooden spoon in the bowl meant that no knives or sharp edges would be allowed in the land, for this would lead to bloodshed. This agreement is still remembered by the two nations today.[26]

This peace treaty was confirmed with wampum at Lake Superior in 1840.[27]

The concept of peaceful relations was linked to a commitment to share lands and resources, which was portrayed through the imagery of the "dish with one spoon"[28] or *Gidoo-naaganinaam*, "Our Dish."[29]

> By conjoining their lands into a common bowl, treaty partners eliminated one of the most frequent causes of conflict and distrust between the tribal peoples of Indigenous North America: competition for hunting grounds and resources. But in agreeing to this act of commitment, they did much more: They obligated themselves to act as relatives toward each other in times of crisis or need. Each could be trusted and relied on steadfastly by the other.[30]   *peace treaties*

Although warfare was a regular occurrence between the Anishinabe of southern Manitoba and the Sioux (Dakota), who occupied the territory immediately west and south,[31] peace was also secured between them through protocols and treaties, including the Peace of Fort Garry.[32] These relationships of peace, centred around the use of territory, continued to be brokered even up to the time of Treaty One. At this time, the United States government was trying to force the Dakota to settle on reserves; many resisted and this led to many Dakota fleeing to Canadian territory.

Alliance provided for sharing between nations in times of need and linked one to the other in order to secure mutual obligation and assistance.[33] After centuries of interconnection between Indigenous peoples on Turtle Island, it was a natural extension of Indigenous diplomatic principles to enter into peace, alliance, and sharing relationships with newcomers:

> Treaty making fulfilled what tribal Indians regarded as a sacred obligation to extend their relationships of connection to all of the different peoples of the world. A treaty was therefore far more than just a reassuring way of blunting contradictions and conflicts of interests between societies. Indians understood a treaty as another way of reconstituting a society itself on an unstable and conflict-ridden multicultural frontier.[34]

The Fur Trade Treaties

In addition to peace treaties, various Indigenous nations from across Canada participated in an extended inter-tribal trading system, rooted in complex systems of tribal diplomacy.[35] These regulated systems of trade be-tween Indigenous peoples directly informed the development of a system of trade in furs with the Europeans. Trade relationships were conducted in large part in accordance with Indigenous protocols, to which the fur trad-ers became accustomed and which they found to be necessary in solidify-ing their trade alliances. John Long, in his book *Treaty No. 9*, refers to the use of the protocols used to solidify the trade relationships: in particular, gift giving, feasting, and the smoking of the pipe.

> Indigenous trading "captains" were presented with suits of clothing, along with gifts of food and alcohol; in return, the HBC factor re-ceived a token gift of furs. Only after more smoking and more speech-es could the winter's furs be bartered for the Company's trade goods. . . . The trade and its attendant ceremonies lasted just a few days, and then the Indigenous visitors left for their winter territories.[36]

The Anishinabe were one of the fur trade's earliest and most important part-ners, trading first with the French, and later with the HBC, the North West Company, and other independent traders. Although the fur trade began along the shores of Hudson Bay, to which many Indigenous nations travelled to trade with the company, in later years, the HBC and its competitors began to travel inland and set up fur trade posts along rivers. Anishinabe control over the inland route to the west and their abundant fur resources required the traders to develop solid relationships with the Anishinabe, who acted as fur providers, guides, and middlemen in the trade with the Cree and Assini-boine further west. In some cases, the alliances ran deep, including connec-tions through marriage between Indigenous women and fur traders.[37]

> They entered into treaties with the Indian tribes and nations, and car-ried on a lucrative and extensive fur trade with the natives. Neither the French government, nor any of its colonists or their trading as-sociations, ever attempted, during an intercourse of over two hun-dred years, to subvert or modify the laws and usages of the aboriginal tribes, except where they had established colonies and permanent settlements, and, then only by persuasion. . . .[38]

While some argue that the fur trade was characterized as an era of depen-dency by the Indigenous people on the fur traders, those assumptions are nuanced in the work of Arthur Ray[39] and in Richard White's *The Middle Ground*,[40] and explained more fully by scholars such as Jennifer Brown, Laura Peers, J. R. Miller, Sylvia Van Kirk, Bruce White, Janna Promislow, and others. In *The Middle Ground*, Richard White argues that a unique world, defined by shared meanings and practices, developed out of the fur trade in the Great Lakes area.[41] "In this world the older worlds of the Algonquians and of various Europeans overlapped, and their mixture created new systems of meaning and of exchange."[42] White further states that a system of legal interaction developed between the Crown and the Anishinabe for the purposes of making treaties of peace and alliance, arguing that "the central and defining aspect of the middle ground was the willingness of those who created it to justify their own actions in terms of what they perceived to be their partner's cultural premises."[43] Janna Promislow argues that this does not mean that they perceived their partners' cultural premises "completely or correctly."[44]

Contact between the Anishinabe and the fur traders came later in the territory of Treaty One than with other Anishinabe further east, with the first fur trading post, Fort Maurepas, being established on the banks of the Winnipeg River, near Lake Winnipeg, in 1734. The Anishinabe of south-eastern Manitoba participated actively in inland fur trade expeditions from the mid-eighteenth century until the decline of the fur trade a century later. Having joined the fur trade in an area of significant competition between traders, both English and French, the Anishinabe of Treaty One likely did not develop "new systems of meaning" to the same extent as Richard White argues was the case for the Great Lakes area between 1650 and 1815, but rather were dealt with more in accordance with Anishinabe requirements and protocols. While attempts were made at various times to assert jurisdiction and import British law into the territory, there was no effective jurisdiction over the Anishinabe.

When the Royal Charter of 1670[45] was granted to the Hudson's Bay Company, ostensibly providing it with exclusive trading rights over the entire Hudson Bay drainage basin,[46] it allowed the HBC to enact laws for "good government of its territory" and to adjudicate company personnel according to the laws of England. These laws were applied only to HBC personnel and not to the Indigenous population that was within the territory described in the Charter. The scope of the jurisdiction of the HBC and the extent of the application of the HBC Charter in the territory (known as Rupert's Land and the Northwestern Territories) was a source of continuous uncertainty. For example, it was unclear whether the HBC Charter or the laws of Canada applied in Rupert's Land and the Northwest Territories after the *Royal Proclamation of 1763*.[47] The *Canada Jurisdiction Act*[48] was passed in 1803 in an attempt to resolve this issue, although the uncertainty continued.[49]

Throughout the fur trade era, the relationships between the fur traders and the Anishinabe were in large part based on Indigenous legal traditions.[50] Over the course of two centuries, a culture of trade treaties, based in part on Anishinabe laws, developed into a template for interaction with Europeans:

> From the 1500s onward, many European individuals submitted themselves to Indigenous legal orders. For example, many traders and explorers adopted Indigenous legal traditions and participated in their laws. A perusal of the fur trade literature reveals that commercial transactions were often conducted in accordance with Indigenous traditions. The giving of gifts, the extension of credit, and the standards of trade were often based on Indigenous legal concepts. Traditionally, Aboriginal peoples in Canada did not transfer goods by conducting their relations with other people in a static way. Relationships were continually renewed and reaffirmed through ceremonial customs. The idea of trade terms being "frozen" through a contract, written on paper, was an alien concept. The traders recognized this fact and conducted their affairs in accordance with Indigenous laws. In the more personal sphere, many of the early marriage relationships between Indigenous women and European men were formed according to Indigenous legal traditions. There were no priests or ministers in the Northwest to officiate at weddings until 1818, and this meant that governing laws were found in the various Indigenous nations throughout the land.[51]

The relationships between fur traders and the Anishinabe were essential to the success of the fur trade. In particular, during the period of increased competition prior to the amalgamation of the HBC and the North West Company in 1821, there was a great deal of deference toward the Anishinabe approach to trade. The traders quickly understood that they were dependent on the Indigenous peoples for the provision of furs, as well as for their knowledge of the land, and thus accommodated the political and trade norms of the Anishinabe. "Because of the fur trade, the tribes of eastern North America during the Encounter era were often treated in fact, if not wholly regarded in theory, as political, economic, and military equals by their European trading partners."[52] Even while engaged in the fur trade, the Anishinabe of Manitoba continued to disperse and hunt in the winter months and then come together again in spring for ceremonies and preparation for the summer harvest. "European traders simply fit into the accustomed annual cycle when they exchanged European goods for furs and food. Trade did not result in Aboriginal dependence on Europeans."[53] When the Anishinabe did meet with the fur traders, Anishinabe protocols were followed. "European fur-trading enterprises learned very quickly to accommodate First Nations wishes and practices, including the web of customs that concerned creating and maintaining harmonious relationships."[54] Gifts were exchanged, the pipe ceremony was conducted, the parties feasted, and alliances were reaffirmed. According to Promislow, "trading practices had evolved to include pipe smoking, speeches, gifts of tobacco, and feasts for the leaders, who then shared the food with their followers. . . . [F]easts and gifts of food were an important part of cementing the relationship between the local Indians and the HBC, quite apart from questions of subsistence and need."[55]

All these protocols were conducted in order to "set the table" for the trade discussions. Each of the protocols had a particular significance, and was viewed as essential to the conduct of good relationships. For example, gift giving created good will between the parties, which would allow the message to flow. "An important message not accompanied by a gift, in the language of Indian diplomacy, was not even worth listening to."[56] Fur traders were incorporated into the system of kinship alliance by adoption or by marriage.[57] Their integration into the Anishinabe kinship structure solidified their roles and obligations both at micro (individual and family) and macro (corporate and national) levels. Such kinship alliances helped secure and clarify the obligations between parties.[58]

J. R. Miller supports Jean Friesen's view that the HBC trading practices affected the process and outcome of the numbered treaty negotiations. Miller argues that the trade ceremonies with the HBC aligned with Indigenous beliefs and practices, and that the HBC entered into binding treaties with the Indigenous people as part of fur trade practice by adhering to Indigenous treaty-making protocols to establish commercial relationships. The "whole string of events and practices — the fur trade protocol — constituted the commercial compact. In other words, the relationship established in this was the treaty."[59] Like Friesen, Miller goes on to describe how these "commercial compacts" and social and kinship relationships set the stage for the negotiation of the land treaties in Manitoba, Saskatchewan, and further west.[60] In *Bounty and Benevolence*, Ray, Miller, and Tough[61] also consider the trade relationships and general good will between the Indians and the HBC as significant in informing the protocols and tone of the Treaty One negotiations; they also note that HBC posts were used as the stage for the treaty negotiations. John Long affirms that when Treaty Nine was negotiated in 1905, the traders' ceremonies that were features of the fur trade "were much diminished but likely not forgotten."[62]

The culture of trade treaties, founded on Anishinabe legal principles, was important for the subsequent negotiation of the treaties with the Crown. The negotiation of trade treaties created expectations about the development of relationships between parties. Trade treaties confirmed respect and adherence to Anishinabe protocols and Anishinabe *inaakonigewin* (law) and acknowledged the procedural and substantive content of those laws:

> At the height of the fur trade, the Western Anishinaabeg lived within a complex cultural middle ground that was neither entirely indigenous Anishinaabe nor foreign European; it was nevertheless uniquely Anishinaabe.[63]

In Commissioner Robinson's report of the 1850s Robinson-Huron and Robinson-Superior treaty negotiations, he acknowledged "the valuable assistance afforded me by all the officers of the Honorable the Hudson's Bay Company resident on the lakes; and the prompt manner in which their Governor, Sir George Simpson, kindly placed their services at my disposal."[64] Treaty One, negotiated at the Stone Fort (Lower Fort Garry), was built upon existing relationships of trust developed in the context of the fur trade which dated back over two centuries:

> The Indians of Canada have, owing to the manner in which they were dealt with for generations by the Hudson's Bay Company, the former rulers of these vast territories, and abiding confidence in the Government of the Queen, or the Great Mother, as they style her. This must not, at all hazards, be shaken.[65]

This practice continued throughout the negotiation of the numbered treaties in western Canada.

Anishinabe Treaties with the Crown

Treaty relationships between and among Indigenous people, as well as treaties with fur traders, served as important precedents for treaties between the Anishinabe and the Crown. The use of Anishinabe laws, both procedural and substantive, informed the earlier treaties and infused the relationship with the Crown. The treaties with the Crown, negotiated over the course of the century preceding Treaty One, adopted Anishinabe methods of concluding treaties and solidified the foundations of the relationship between the Anishinabe and the Crown.

Other Indigenous nations formed treaty relationships with both the French Crown and later the British Crown. The earliest recorded example of treaty making between Indigenous peoples and a European power on Turtle Island is the agreement between the Haudenosaunee and the Dutch in 1613. The Haudenosaunee Two Row Wampum Belt (*Guswhenta* or *Kaswehnta*) confirmed the relationship between the two nations and depicts the two separate paths (or rivers) on which each party travels in its own vessel:

> The *Gus-Wen-Tah* is comprised of a bed of white wampum shell beads symbolizing the sacredness and purity of the treaty agreement between the two sides. Two parallel rows of purple wampum beads that extend down the length of the belt represent the separate paths traveled by the two sides on the same river. Each side travels in its own vessel: the Indians in a birch bark canoe, representing their laws, customs and ways, and the whites in a ship, representing their laws, customs, and ways. In presenting the *Gus-Wen-Tah* to solemnize their treaties with the Western colonial powers, the Iroquois would explain its basic underlying vision of law and peace between different peoples as follows: We shall each travel the river together, side by side, but in our own boat. Neither of us will steer the other's vessel.[66]

The alliances between the Haudenosaunee and the Dutch, and later between the Haudenosaunee and the British (referred to as the Covenant Chain), laid the foundations that informed all future alliances and relationships between the French Crown and the Indigenous peoples of Canada and later with the British Crown. The Anishinabe had direct relationships with the British Crown as early as the 1700s. Treaties were concluded between the Great Lakes Anishinabek[67] and the French, according to Anishinabe ceremonies, protocols, and wampum.[68] The relationship between the Anishinabe and the Crown further developed after the capitulation of France in North America in 1761. Under the terms of capitulation, Indigenous lands were to be protected and the Indigenous peoples were not to be punished for assisting the French in the war.[69] The Anishinabe were clear with the British Crown representative that, although the French had been conquered, the Anishinabe had not.[70] Williams argues that "there was a time when the West had to listen seriously to these indigenous tribal visions of how different peoples might live together in relationships of trust, solidarity, and respect."[71]

In 1763, the British Crown issued a royal proclamation which protected Indian lands from occupation, settlement, or sale without their consent.[72] Under the *Royal Proclamation of 1763*, surrenders and purchases could only be made by the Crown according to a specified process.[73] John Borrows argues that First Nations, including many tribes of Anishinabe, were active participants in the formulation and ratification of the *Royal Proclamation*. In 1764, the Treaty of Niagara assembled over 2,000 chiefs of 24 nations, from as far away as Hudson Bay, for the negotiation of a treaty of alliance and peace. This was also an opportunity to "brighten the chain" of agreements concluded with the British Crown in years prior to the Niagara gathering. Although many Anishinabe chiefs attended at Niagara, it is unclear whether the Anishinabe people who later negotiated Treaty One were represented among the 2,000 chiefs in attendance. It would be safe to assume that, even if they were not in direct attendance, they would have had knowledge of the meeting and the treaty that was concluded with the Crown.

The *Proclamation* and the Treaty of Niagara set the terms for the relationship between the Crown and Indigenous people, and set the stage for the negotiations of the future treaties. "The purpose of the Treaty conference was for the chiefs to discuss the principles that would govern their relationship with the British sovereign. The chiefs' role was jurisdictional; they watched over the territories and settled disputes."[74] The Covenant Chain Belt[75] was presented by the British Crown, and some have indicated that a Two Row Wampum Belt was presented by the Indigenous nations.

Copies of the *Royal Proclamation* were distributed by the Crown. "This agreement, at the start of the formal relationship between the British and the First Nations of Canada, demonstrates the foundation-building principles of peace, friendship, and respect agreed to between the parties."[76]

According to Sa'ke'j Henderson, the Niagara treaty was a consensual relationship of peace, protection, and respect, with each member of the "Ojibway Confederacy"[77] being treated "as sovereign nations with treaty capacity."[78] Henderson further states that the Two Row Wampum Belt, which was presented by the Anishinabe to the Crown, expressed sovereignty and non-interference, principles that were foundational to Anishinabe treaty relationships.[79] The 1764 Niagara treaty created the context for future treaty negotiations between the Crown and the Anishinabe. According to Borrows, "the express terms and promises made in the Proclamation and at Niagara may yet be found to form the underlying terms and conditions which should be implied in all subsequent and future treaties."[80]

The Covenant Chain Belt, the Two Row Wampum Belts, and the *Royal Proclamation* were each invoked in many instances after the 1760s in the context of treaty negotiations, including in 1818 on Lake Huron and at the Manitoulin Island treaty negotiations in the 1860s. Mark Walters finds that in "subsequent treaty councils, chiefs would hold the same belt in their hands, recite the story of the meeting at Niagara and implore 'our Great Father' — the king — to honour the promises then made."[81] The Anishinabe recalled what Sir W. Johnson had said at the Niagara treaty:

> Children, you must all touch this Belt of Peace. I touch it myself, that we may all be brethren united, and hope our friendship will never cease. I will call you my children; we will send warmth (presents) to your country; and your families shall never be in want. Look towards the rising sun. My Nation is as brilliant as it is, and its word cannot be violated. . . . If you should ever require my assistance, send this Belt, and my hand will be immediately stretched forth to assist you.[82]

This is an example of what Williams refers to as the "distinctive language of multicultural diplomacy that Indians and Europeans used to conduct their treaty relations with each other."[83]

In the century following the *Royal Proclamation* and the Treaty of Niagara, many other treaties were negotiated between the Crown and Anishinabe in what is now Ontario. These treaties furthered the relationships that had been forged between the Anishinabe and the Crown. In the treaty purchases of land in southern Ontario, the Anishinabe were continuously reassured that they could continue to use the land as they always had, without modification to the terms of the original treaty. The Robinson-Huron and Robinson-Superior treaties (1850) set aside large reserves and confirmed the right to continue hunting and fishing, although there was discomfort among the Anishinabe about the approach to settlement and their subsequent displacement. The Manitoulin Island treaties (1861–62) achieved only a partial "surrender of land," as some Anishinabe refused to sign the treaties on the basis that they still had title to their land.[84] The same year that Treaty One was negotiated marked the last year that treaties were negotiated with Indian tribes in the United States. Although the United States government continued to make "agreements" with tribes,[85] the shift in policy was certainly dramatic and had a ripple effect, which likely was felt across the border into the Treaty One area.

Anishinabe treaty making with the Crown was a well-established practice by 1871, in the Upper Canada treaties, the Robinson-Huron treaties, and the United States treaties. Each of the treaties between the Anishinabe and the Crown "set the table" for the negotiation of Treaty One. Each of the negotiations built upon the principles established in the *Royal Proclamation* and at the Niagara treaty, and was conducted, at least in part, in accordance with Anishinabe protocols and laws:

> Treaties were clearly not static agreements from an Anishinaabe perspective but were contingent on each nation meeting the obligations they carried. These commitments necessitated a constant renewal of friendship and peace throughout their fulfillment. Anishinaabe nations, when entering into a treaty with the United States and Canada, frequently built upon their previous agreements.[86]

The non-interference and mutual assistance that are illustrated by the Covenant Chain Belt and the Two Row Wampum Belts help further illustrate the perspective that the Anishinabe brought to the treaty and the mutual reliance of the treaty parties on the Anishinabe procedural and substantive legal principles that informed Treaty One.

Conclusion

Prior to Treaty One, there was an established history of inter-nation[87] and trade law that existed, distinct from European or Canadian laws. Robert Williams, Jr. and Richard White argue that this resulted in a newly developed system of law, founded on Indigenous legal principles:

> The Encounter era treaty tradition recalls the long-neglected fact in . . . history that there was a time in our national experience when Indians tried to create a new type of society with Europeans on the multicultural frontier of colonial North America. Recovering this shared legal world is crucial to the task of reconstructing our shared understandings of the sources and the nature of the rights belonging to Indian peoples.[88]

According to Henderson, there were existing Indigenous orders into which the immigrants attempted to fit themselves, which "generated a common jurisdictional and institutional framework of legal pluralism."[89] Others view Indigenous normative principles not simply as contributing factors to the legal relationships, but as being the pillars of those relationships. Regardless of which view one takes, the fact is that Indigenous values were taken into account in treaty making long before the negotiation of Treaty One. The application of these principles extended to relationships among Indigenous nations, to relationships with fur trade partners, and to treaties with other nations, including Britain, France, and later Canada.

Given this political and geographic context, questions arise as to the application of British colonial law by the Hudson's Bay Company from 1670 to 1870, Canadian law after 1870, and Manitoban provincial law as of 1870. Gerald Friesen argues that when Manitoba became a province in 1870, there was a new, jointly developed legal order in place.[90] It is unclear what system of state law would apply in the territory of Treaty One at the time of the negotiations in 1871, given the recent shift in "ownership" of the territory from a company to the Canadian state and the creation of the province, all in the months preceding the treaty negotiation. Furthermore, the Treaty One lands extended beyond the 1870 Manitoba border into the adjacent timber lands.

There are questions as to whether there was any *de facto* jurisdiction over the Anishinabe of the area prior to Treaty One. Long argues that when

"Rupert's Land, the HBC territory, was acquired by the three-year-old Dominion of Canada in 1870, the Indigenous inhabitants likely understood this transfer to mean (if they were aware of it at all) that Canada would somehow continue the long-established fur trade protocols governing immigrants' interactions with the First Nations."[91]

The issues of consent to use land, as required by the *Royal Proclamation*, had not yet been resolved, and there was no effective imposition of law or jointly developed law prior to the making of the treaty in 1871. Consequently, and in the absence of an imposed or jointly developed system of law, the Anishinabe relied on *inaakonigewin* to inform their understanding in the negotiation of Treaty One.

CHAPTER TWO

Manito Api — this "Piece of Land":
Treaty Making with the Indians of Manitoba

The Selkirk Treaty

As expansion and settlement was moving westward through Ontario in the nineteenth century, the region that is now Manitoba continued to be relatively undeveloped. One notable exception was the Selkirk Settlement, established via a land grant from the Hudson's Bay Company to Lord Selkirk in the early nineteenth century. In order to secure the "quiet possession" of a two-mile reserve on the banks of the Red River, Lord Selkirk negotiated a treaty with the Anishinabe chiefs of the region in 1817, the Selkirk Treaty. The Selkirk Treaty was concluded with many of the same Anishinabe bands[1] that would later negotiate Treaty One.[2]

The Selkirk Treaty had been made to settle disputes between the incoming settlers and the Anishinabe and Cree over use of land for settlement and agriculture. Lord Selkirk noted "their resentment against my settlers for having taken possession of their lands without their consent or any purchase from them."[3] Selkirk then brokered an agreement that allowed for the use of two-mile tracts on each side of the Red and Assiniboine Rivers. He reasoned that the purchase of land for significant goods could potentially bring into question the validity of a sale; he therefore chose to negotiate for the exclusive use of land, not in terms of a sale or surrender, but rather as a "gift":

> If a large quantity of goods were offered for the purchase it might be said that the temptation of immediate advantage had induced them to sacrifice their permanent interests. I would therefore propose to them merely a small annual present in the nature of a quit rent or acknowledgement of their right: — and having specified what I intend

to give in this way I would leave it to themselves to specify the boundaries of the lands which they agree to give up on that consideration
and to appropriate to me for the exclusive use of the settlers.[4]

The intent of the treaty was later disputed, as the Anishinabe claimed that
the land had been leased while the HBC claimed the land as purchased
from the Indians. Chief Peguis affirmed that their land had never been sold
to Selkirk or to the HBC:

> We never sold our land to the said Company, nor to the Earl of Sel-
> kirk; and yet the said Company mark out and sell our lands without
> our permission. Is this right? I and my people do not take their prop-
> erty from them, without giving them great value for it, as furs and
> other things. . . . I got nothing for my land. . . . I speak loud: listen![5]

This treaty experience with Selkirk was influential in shaping the Anishinabe understanding of agreements with settlers for the use of land in what

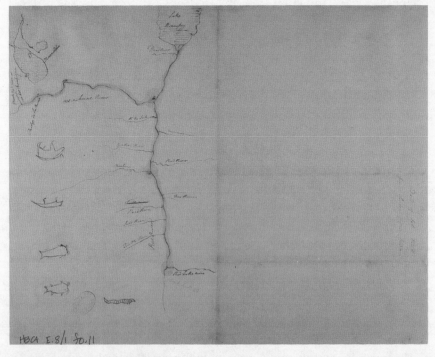

*Map attached to deed of 18 July 1817 conveying land adjoining the Red and
Assiniboine rivers from Indian Chiefs to Lord Selkirk. HBCA E.8/1 fo.11.*

would later become the Treaty One area. In particular, the concept of an annual rent in exchange for the use of land and the idea that jurisdiction over land would be retained by the Anishinabe were concepts that likely carried over into or informed the Anishinabe negotiations at Treaty One.

The Need to Secure Alliance

The time and place of Treaty One is particularly significant to its negotiation and its terms. It was the first of the numbered treaties of Western Canada to be concluded. It was the hinge on which western agricultural expansion, and the national railway, were resting. Various geographic, political, social, and economic factors influenced the Anishinabe and the Crown prior to and around the time of the Treaty One negotiations. Miller points to concerns about food security, intertribal wars, and a succession of epidemics as important contextual factors leading up to the negotiation of the numbered treaties in the 1870s.[6] In particular, the end of the fur trade and the transfer of HBC territorial interests to Canada, the Canadian desire to expand westward and settle the whole of Canada, as well as the creation of the province of Manitoba, all had an impact on how Treaty One was negotiated.[7] In eastern Canada, the Indigenous population was outnumbered by Europeans, but such was not the case in Manitoba.

> In the western interior . . . [f]rom the early 1600s to 1870, the Aboriginal people of prairie Canada lived within a society defined by traditional Aboriginal laws, while Europeans in the region increasingly demanded a justice system for themselves akin to those in Britain and Europe.[8]

In Assiniboia,[9] the Quarterly General Court was established in 1835, and in 1864 it was determined that British law would be applied to the settlers in both criminal and civil cases. Enforcement was constantly a challenge. In his report to the Aboriginal Justice Inquiry of Manitoba, historian Gerry Friesen argued that because of the interaction of the Métis[10] with the White settlers in the mid-nineteenth century "a distinctively Manitoban mix of European and Aboriginal legal cultures was evolving in Red River." It is unclear what, if any, jurisdiction was claimed or exercised with regard to the Anishinabe.

The geographic distance from Canada, the proximity to the United States, the important waterways linking the Red River area to the United States (via the Red River) and Canada (via the Winnipeg River, also known as the "Highway to the West"), as well as the abundant forest and agricultural potential of the prairies made this area highly desirable to Canada, while being just out of reach of Canada's control. In addition, the issue of Indian title had to be settled in order to allow for the distribution of 1.4 million acres of lands to the Métis, in accordance with Manitoba's Constitution.[11] As stated by Marcel Mauss in *The Gift*, Indigenous people, faced with European or White settlers, "may move away or in case of mistrust or defiance they may resort to arms; or else they can come to terms." In this case, the Anishinabe and the Crown attempted to come to terms. "Indians are found coping and responding to Europeans with sophistication, resourcefulness, and long-term vision on the complex cultural landscape of the Encounter era frontier."[12]

With the decline of the fur trade and later the transfer of Rupert's Land and the Northwest Territories to Canada, jurisdictional questions were perpetuated. Canada, newly formed in 1867, was in its infancy as a nation at the time the Treaty One negotiations were undertaken. The Canadian government had assumed jurisdiction over "Indians and Lands Reserved for Indians" under section 91(24) of the *Constitution Act, 1867.* Rupert's Land and the Northwest Territory (formerly referred to as "Indian Country") was transferred to Canada by the British Crown (which had acquired it from the Hudson's Bay Company), on the condition that Canada protect First Nations and reserved Indian lands. Canada proposed to annex Rupert's Land and the Northwest Territories as new territories of Canada. As Canada prepared to assume control over these new territories, their surveying efforts were met with opposition from the Métis of Red River, who would not let Governor William McDougall enter the territory:

> The government had not consulted those who already lived in the area, most of whom were First Nations and Métis people, but sent surveyors to the Red River to prepare for a new system of land distribution, even before the transfer to Canada was complete. Métis people, who felt their land holdings threatened, ordered the surveyors to cease their activities and organized a common response with other residents to the incursions of the government of Canada.[13]

Historian W. L. Morton qualifies the Red River situation of 1869–70 as a resistance rather than a rebellion, because of the power vacuum that existed in the Red River at the time.[14] According to Gerald Friesen, "without the presence of troops in Red River, HBC law depended on the consent of Rupert's Land Residents."[15]

The Métis formed a provisional government and negotiated Manitoba's terms of entry into the Canadian confederation. It was agreed that the Red River area was to enter into confederation as a partner province, known

Chief Peguis, who had made the Treaty with Lord Selkirk in 1817, was instrumental in voicing the concerns and desires of the Anishinabe in declarations and statements, including to newspapers, government officials, and directly to the Queen. Archives of Manitoba, Peguis 1 (N17188)

as Manitoba. Louis Riel called the agreement a "treaty" between "nations." The *Manitoba Act*[16] came into force on May 12, 1870, and provided that 1.4 million acres of land would be set aside for the use of the children of Métis heads of families. No negotiations or discussions took place with the Anishinabe.

As settlement increased, the issue of Indigenous title to the land had to be resolved, as required by the *Royal Proclamation*. In addition, the Anishinabe chiefs requested of the Lieutenant-Governor that a treaty be negotiated, and that matters of interest to them be resolved,[17] as more and more settlers were entering their territory and using their resources. "Ojibwa governments were not prepared to give up their lands, on which they depended for their livelihood, without a formal relationship that would protect and respect their jurisdiction, lands and resources."[18] As early as 1857, Chief Peguis petitioned the Aborigines' Protection Society in England, stating that before settlers enter Anishinabe territory and "take possession of our lands, we wish that a fair and mutually advantageous treaty be entered into with my tribe."[19] The Anishinabe recognized that the Lieutenant-Governor had authority over the settler population, but not over them.

Following the Métis resistance in Manitoba in 1869–70, in which the citizens of Red River protested the purchase of Rupert's Land and the transfer to Canada, it was clear that the Indigenous populations in western Canada were a strong force that the Government of Canada had great difficulty controlling from afar. There was significant Indian unrest following the end of the HBC rule, the Red River resistance, and the influx of White settlers.

> [T]he Hudson's Bay Company — had for long years, been eminently successful in securing the good-will of the Indians — but on their sway, coming to an end, the Indian mind was disturbed. The events, that transpired in the Red River region, in the years 1869–1870, during the period when a provisional government was attempted to be established, had perplexed the Indians. They moreover, had witnessed a sudden irruption into the country of whites from without.[20]

On behalf of the residents of Red River, Louis Riel's list of grievances to Canada had included a demand for Indian treaties.[21]

The Anishinabe were well aware of changing circumstances and the need to negotiate a peaceful agreement in relation to the land. Despite past treaties,[22] Anishinabe land tenure in what had in 1870 become the province of Manitoba was not as secure as they would have liked.[23] The Indians "were full of uneasiness, owing to the influx of population, denied the validity of the Selkirk Treaty, and had in some instances obstructed settlers and surveyors."[24]

Reigning Uncertainty

In 1868, the Portage band had warded off settlers who were taking timber from their lands. The Hon. James McKay[25] was sent to negotiate a three-year agreement with Chief Yellow Quill (the Rat Creek Treaty),[26] in anticipation of a full treaty.[27] Indians further west restricted all access to their territories: "[T]he natives around Riding Mountain (the finest region in the country) have distinctly forbidden anyone to approach their territory until the treaty has been consummated."[28] Those in the immediate area of settlement, such as Chief Peguis and his son Henry Prince, published an "Indian Manifesto" in *The Nor'Wester* newspaper declaring that anyone who cultivated Indian land would have to make annual payment as acknowledgement of the Indians' title to the land.

During the winter prior to the Treaty One negotiations, Chief Moosoos of High Bluff wrote to the Lieutenant-Governor, complaining that settlers had been cutting wood in his territory. He included with his letter a written warning and posted notices on the land forbidding the settlers from cutting wood:

> Whereas the Indians' title to all lands west of the fifty mile boundary line at High Bluff had not been extinguished and whereas these lands are being taken up and the wood thereon cut off by parties who have no right or title thereto, I hereby warn all such parties that they are fringing [sic] on lands that as yet virtually belong to the Indians.[29]

In the spring of 1871, a council of 73 principal headman of Portage La Prairie met and issued written resolutions protecting their land from settler encroachment:

> Why we pass these resolutions at our council held today is because that we never have yet, seen or received anything for the land and the woods that belong to us, and the settlers use to enrich themselves. We

might not have felt so hard at the present at the usage we have rec'd of late, had we ever rec'd any remuneration for the said lands and woods that rightly belong to us. *So we feel fully justified in passing these laws amongst ourselves and for our own protection.*"[30]

The settlers were uneasy about the uncertainty that reigned in the absence of a treaty with the Crown, as required by the *Royal Proclamation*. The hope was that a treaty would be concluded speedily.[31] At the idea of a temporary and tentative treaty, *The Manitoban* published an editorial that bemoaned delay and uncertainty. "The Indians are confident that now a permanent treaty is to be made, and are ready to make it; why then not make it at once, and have done with it? . . . Why keep the Settlement in suspense; why place the lives of the people in jeopardy by such tardiness; and why leave the great impediment to immigration removed?"[32]

Given the political instability and Métis resistance of 1869–70 and Canada's obvious inability to control the Red River Colony, Rupert's Land and the Northwest Territories and its population, Canada as a new nation was vulnerable and required the "peace and goodwill" of the Anishinabe. The Treaty Commissioner was given instructions to communicate with Indian bands for the purposes of securing friendly relations for travel and settlement, including the system employed by the HBC in dealing with them previously.[33]

Upon his appointment and arrival in western Canada, Adams Archibald, the Lieutenant-Governor of Manitoba and the Northwest Territories, met with the Anishinabe in the fall of 1870. Archibald reported that "the Indians were anxiously awaiting my arrival, and were much excited on the subject of their lands being occupied without attention being first given to their claims for compensation."[34] Archibald promised to make a treaty with them the following year and sent them home with ammunition "to enable [them] to gain a livelihood during the winter by hunting."[35] In 1871, Wemyss Simpson was appointed Indian Commissioner by the Privy Council of Canada because of "the necessity of arranging with the bands of Indians inhabiting the tract of country between Thunder Bay and the Stone Fort, for the cession, subject to certain reserves such as they should select, of the lands occupied by them."[36] As he explained to the Indians gathered at the Stone Fort:

It is now nearly thirty years since I came first among you, and I have taken a great deal of interest in you ever since. . . . Within the last four years I have sat in Parliament of the Queen, in Ottawa, and ever since I have held that position, I have tried to impress on the Government of the Queen the great necessity that existed for her to treat with all her Red subjects, and make some kind of arrangement by which they would understand exactly the position they held in this Territory for the future.[37]

Despite his assurances that he had "been present at a great many Indian treaties in Canada," Simpson had been unsuccessful in securing the treaty with the Anishinabe at the North-West Angle in July of 1871.[38] Following his first unsuccessful attempt, and under pressure to conclude a treaty during the summer of 1871, Simpson continued on to Manitoba, where he met with Lieutenant-Governor Archibald and other officials, including James McKay. Collectively, they agreed to treat with the Indians of the province and for lands beyond the boundaries of the province "as were required for immediate entry and use."[39] Simpson issued proclamations to meet on July 25 at Lower Fort Garry and August 17 at Manitoba Post. The Commissioner knew that these treaties would set the stage for the future treaties that would open up western Canada to settlement, and to the national railway:

I look upon the proceedings, we are now initiating, as important in their bearing upon our relations to the Indians of the whole continent. In fact, the terms we now agree upon will probably shape the arrangements we shall have to make with all the Indians between the Red River and the Rocky Mountains. It will therefore be well to neglect nothing that is within our power to enable us to start fairly with the negotiations.[40]

Knowing that political relations with the Indians were of great significance to Canada, the Commissioner undertook the "work, of obtaining their good will, by entering into treaties of alliance with them."[41]

PART 2

MAKING THE STONE FORT TREATY

CHAPTER THREE

The Anishinabe at the Stone Fort:
The People who Belong to this Land

In this chapter, I turn to the *ode* (heart) of the treaty: the treatment of land. The detailed story of the Treaty One negotiations on land issues is complex and, at critical points, obscure. We see in the following account that competing understandings of land and their foundation in the conceptions of each party were expressed both explicitly in the record and implicitly throughout the entire negotiations. This chapter therefore takes the form of a narrative, working through the negotiations, using the written record, telling the story of the process and substance of treaty making.

In the summer of 1871, more than 1,000 Indian men, accompanied by women and children, assembled at the Stone Fort to make a treaty. They were joined by their Métis cousins and some of the local settlers, who all wished to know "the policy of the government"[1] in relation to the "quieting of Indian title"[2] in Manitoba and the adjoining timber districts. The *odenong* (geographic heart) of the continent was filled with instability and uncertainty due to the influx of settlers, Britain's sale of the west to Canada, the Métis Resistance of 1869–70, and the creation of the province of Manitoba just a year earlier.

Based on the uncertainty of title and the oftentimes tenuous relationships between settlers and Indians in relation to land, the consensus was that issues of land and access to resources needed to be dealt with urgently; thus, negotiations were entered into. These negotiations were largely based on Anishinabe protocols and practices, as had been employed in past treaty and fur trade relationships.

Treaty One was made at Lower Fort Garry, a Hudson's Bay Company fur trading post, also known as the Stone Fort, between the Anishinabe of southern Manitoba and the Crown. Although the Swampy Cree are men-

48

tioned as parties to the treaty, they essentially consisted of a small group who were living on the St. Peter's reserves with the Anishinabe, under the leadership of Chief Peguis (who had entered into the Selkirk Treaty on behalf of his band) and later his son, Henry Prince. The treaty negotiations had assembled Anishinabe from the Red River area as far south as the U.S. border, and east along the Winnipeg River, and those inhabiting most of what had recently become the Province of Manitoba.[3]

After a long winter of waiting for the negotiations, the terms of the relationship were worked out over nine days, in conditions of both rain and sun. The Anishinabe camp housed over 100 tents, assembled in a semi-circle outside the fort, with the Chiefs' lodges at the centre and fires for each. There was a relaxed atmosphere in the camp as the Anishinabe continued their activities and interactions, including cooking, visiting, and gambling:

> Of the followers it must be said that they are apparently very comfortable. Most of their lodges are of birch bark, but a considerable number have good tents. Each lodge or tent has a fire in front or inside, where the Indian women are ever-lastingly baking bread or making tea. Any number of horses and dogs roam through the camp, and along in the afternoons one or more large crowds gathered near the tents; the sound of a tambourine, or the noise of a person hammering a frying pan with a piece of wood, accompanied by two or three persons chanting in a low tone, proclaim that gambling is going forward. A near approach to one of these groups will show the gamblers playing the moccasin game, or some other, with the stakes — generally clothing — lying close at hand.[4]

The negotiations themselves took place outside the fort, with the Commissioner and Lieutenant-Governor seated under an awning, facing the Chiefs who were seated in chairs. The "Indians moved to meet the Commissioner en masse."[5]

On the first day of negotiations, Lieutenant-Governor Archibald opened the discussion by recalling his promise made to the Anishinabe the previous fall, to enter into a treaty with the Queen. "I promised that in the spring you would be sent for, and that either I, or some person directly appointed to represent your Great Mother, should be here to meet you, and notice would be given you when to convene at this place to talk over what was right to be done."[6] Henry Prince had been the most insistent to have the treaty made. He and his members, from St. Peter's Indian Settlement, were the most numerous group present at the negotiations. Prince recalled his loyalty to the Queen and recounted his refusal to participate in the Red River Resistance the previous year: "[A]ll last winter I worked for the Queen. . . . My people had nothing to do with it and no dark-skinned man had anything whatever to do with it."[7] Archibald commended the Anishinabe for not participating in the resistance, on behalf of the Queen: "[S]he had been very glad to see that you had acted during the troubles like good and true children of your Great Mother."[8]

The son of Chief Peguis, Henry Prince, negotiated Treaty One on behalf of his people. Archives of Manitoba, Prince, H. 1 (N10501).

The Negotiations

Assurances of Non-interference

The negotiations began with statements by both the Lieutenant-Governor and the Commissioner assuring the Indians that they could continue to use their traditional territories for hunting, trapping, fishing, and other harvesting, as they had done in the past. While the treaty was meant to ensure that the land in question could be used by settlers for agriculture, the amount of land used for this purpose was to be limited. Assurances were made that Indian ways of life would be sustained. Further assurances were made that Indians would not be confined to reserves, but could choose to live on them if they wished to farm:

> When you have made your treaty you will still be free to hunt over much of the land included in the treaty. Much of it is rocky and unfit for cultivation, much of it that is wooded is beyond the place where the white man will require to go, at all events for some time to come. Till these lands are needed for use you will be free to hunt over them, and make all the use of them which you have made in the past. But when lands are needed to be tilled or occupied, you must not go on them any more. There will still be plenty of land that is neither tilled nor occupied where you can go and roam and hunt as you have always done, and if you wish to farm, you will go to your own reserve where you will find a place ready for you to live on and cultivate.[9]

Archibald and Simpson expressed the Queen's wishes for the happiness of her children. They assured the Anishinabe that the Queen would not force them to adopt White ways, nor would she interfere in their existing ways:

> She would like them to adopt the habits of the whites — to till land and raise food, and store it up against a time of want. She thinks this would be the best thing for her Red Children to do, that it would make them safer from famine and sickness, and make their homes more comfortable. But the Queen, though she may think it good for you to adopt civilized habits, has no idea of compelling you to do so. This she leaves to your own choice, and *you need not live like the white man unless you can be persuaded to do so with your own free will.*[10]

In the face of assurances that Anishinabe ways of life would continue, and that opportunities to farm would be made available to them, if so desired, the Anishinabe "declared that they would never again raise their voice against the enforcement of the law . . . ."[11]

The opening of the negotiations was marked by assurances that Indian ways of life would continue, but, more importantly, that they would not be interfered with by the Queen or her other subjects. Retention of autonomy, jurisdiction, and sovereignty over their actions was essential in securing the agreement with the Anishinabe.

Reserves — Ishkonigan: What Was Set Aside for Ourselves

The commissioners explained that the Queen proposed to set aside, in perpetuity, land for the Indians to cultivate, "should the chase fail," in the form of reserves. The Queen would ensure that those lands were kept, for use by the Indians and their children forever, without intrusion by White settlers. It would be a place to pitch a camp, build a house, and engage in agriculture, at the Indians' pleasure:

> Your Great Mother, therefore, will lay aside for you "lots" of land to be used by you and your children forever. She will not allow the white man to intrude upon these lots. She will make rules to keep them for you, so that as long as the sun shall shine, there shall be no Indian who has not a place that he can call his home, where he can go and pitch his camp, or if he chooses, build his house and till his land.[12]

The Anishinabe were then asked to select the lands which they would want as reserves but "when their answer came it proved to contain demands of such an exorbitant nature, that much time was spent in reducing their terms to a basis upon which an arrangement could be made."[13] It was apparent that there were incompatible understandings of what would be reserved exclusively for the Indians, "they wishing to have two-thirds of the Province as a reserve."[14]

The initial reserve selection was rejected by the Commissioner. "If all these lands are to be reserve, I would like to know what you have to sell?"[15] The Hon. Mr. McKay, "by request of His Excellency and the Commissioner, addressed the Indians, showing them that their demands were so preposterous, that, if granted, they would have scarcely anything to cede, and urging them to curtail their demands."[16] The Lieutenant-Governor also urged the Indians to agree to a treaty now, stating that, if they refused, the offer would not present itself again. In his view, this agreement was superior to what had been offered in the United States to the Indians, who received annuities for only 20 years, not in perpetuity, as was being proposed to the Anishinabe in the Treaty One negotiations. Archibald explained that 160 acres meant a quarter of a square mile of land, and then entered into explanations with diagrams. He reminded the Indians that, "instead of having only the quantity now held by Christian Indian families (3 chains), they should have three times as much, and more reserved to them under the treaty."[17]

The Anishinabe were not easily convinced that the amount of land proposed by the Commissioners could sustain their way of life. It was reiterated to them that the reserves would be for settlement, if they so chose, and that there would be plenty of land to roam and hunt, and if they wished, they could go to their reserve to farm.[18]

Under Threat

Throughout the negotiations, the Commissioner used the implied threat of the influx of White settlers to encourage the Anishinabe to agree to the allotment of 160 acres per family of five:

> We told them that whether they wished it or not, immigrants would come in and fill up the country, that every year from this one twice as many in number as their whole people there assembled would pour into the Province, and in a little while would spread all over it, and that now was the time for them to come to an arrangement that would secure homes and annuities for themselves and their children.[19]

On the third day of negotiations, the Indians were asked if they would accept terms "same as those given Canadian Indians already treated with, [consisting of] a small annuity to each family, to last as long as the sun shines, as much land as is allowed to their brethren in Canada, the reserves to be chosen by the Indians themselves. If they were satisfied with these general terms, the Commission [sic] said he was ready at once to proceed to details."[20]

There was no mention in the general terms of the surrender of land, nor had there been any recorded explanation of what would be given up or surrendered, nor of the concept of surrender itself. The Indians were asked to provide an answer by the Monday (the next day being Sunday, at which time negotiations would be deferred). *The Manitoban* newspaper reported that the "Commissioner also spoke in further elucidation of the benefits to be conferred on the Indians, by entering into the proposed treaty,"[21] without explaining what other benefits were being proposed in addition to what had just been described:

His Excellency also strongly urged on the Indians the advisability of accepting the terms. Their Mother the Queen wished to benefit them — wished to place her red subjects on the same footing as the white, and even went further, in giving to her red subjects what she did not give to the others, an annual bounty to last as long as the sun shone. In the East, the Indians, the Queen's subjects, were living happy and tranquil, enjoying all the rights and privileges of white men, and having homes of their own. What had made them happy the Queen was willing to give her Indian subjects here, and no more. They might at once and forever dismiss from their heads all nonsense about large reserves; for they could not and would not be granted. The matter must be looked at by them like men of common sense, who see the Queen trying to save a home for them; if they refuse her offer, it will not be made to them again. His Excellency further reminded them that the terms offered them were better than those under which white men came to settle and made themselves comfortable homes. In the United States reserves were sometimes given and sometimes withheld, while the annuities generally terminated after 20 years. The annuities offered the Indians in this negotiation would last as long as the sun shines.[22]

Uncertainty

Chief Ayee-ta-pe-pe-tung wanted to understand with more certainty what was being offered, and the limits of the territory about to be treated for. McKay explained that the territory was defined by the limits of the province. The chief then turned to the Commissioner, requesting that he make his offer before the chief would make his. "I want, first, to see what you are offering; and then I'll tell you my offer."[23] The Indians were hesitant. Lieutenant-Governor Archibald wrote, "[A] general acquiescence in the views laid down by Mr. Simpson and myself was expressed but it was quite clear, by the proceedings of to-day, that our views were imperfectly apprehended."[24] Additionally: "A Portage Indian said that what puzzled his band was that they were to be shut up on a small reserve, and only get ten shillings each for the balance. They could not understand it."[25] Archibald expressed his concern in a letter to the Secretary of State, finding that

> the Indians seem to have false ideas of the meaning of a reserve. They had been led to suppose that large tracts of grounds were to be set aside for them as hunting grounds, including timber lands, of which they might sell the wood as if they were proprietors of the soil. I wished to correct this idea at the outset.[26]

The confusion continued throughout the negotiations. On the third day of the negotiations, Wa-sus-koo-koon, representing the Indians between Pembina and Fort Garry, "expressed a desire to know a little more of what

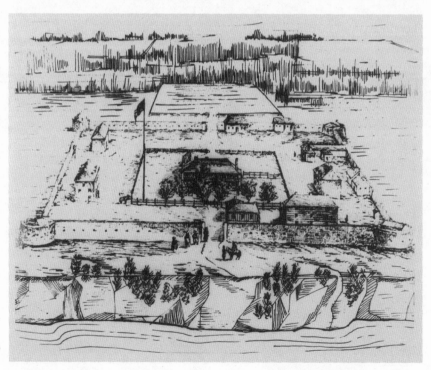

An image of Lower Fort Garry, summer 1871. Archives of Manitoba, Events 243/3 (N13291)

the Queen intended for the Indians." The commissioner explained, "Hon. Mr. McKay, at the request of the Governor and the Indians, also entered into very full explanations in Indian."[27] No detail of what was said is provided in the record.

On the fifth day of proceedings, the Indians were still hesitant. Henry Prince presented a copy of his father Chief Peguis' will and stated, "we have been already four days in this negotiation, and it seems as though it will not be brought to a decision."[28] In response, the commissioner stated that he was "quite ready to finish up matters that day. The delay rested with the Indians altogether."[29] He explained that the terms proposed were now "better terms than are offered to the Canadian Indians, and to those of the United States, and our Indians will not . . . receive the offer we make them."[30] He stated that it would be foolish for the Indians not to accept the offer.

Chief Ka-ma-twa-kau-ness-noo was still unsure, and "wanted to know how the Indians spoken of were dealt with — wanted to hear the ins and outs of everything."[31] Chief Ayee-ta-pe-pe-tung explained that the land in question was his property. He could not see benefit for his children and therefore could not enter into treaty if it would not benefit future generations:

> God gave me this land you are speaking to me about, and it kept me well to this day. I live at the end of the Settlement, in a clean place (unsettled); and as I travelled through the Settlement, I looked on nothing but my property! I saw pieces of land high up (meaning bridges) and these are my property! When I went into the houses by the wayside, these too I considered my property — (laughter).[32]

When Wa-sus-koo-koon asked what would happen if there were more children, the Lieutenant-Governor assured him that when the reserves became too small, they would be sold and the Indians would acquire land elsewhere in the west.

Western Views of Land

At times throughout the negotiations, the Lieutenant-Governor espoused the liberal enlightenment views of the day,[33] namely, that the natural use to which the land should be put was agriculture.[34] "God, he said, intends this land to raise great crops for all his children, and the time has come when it is to be used for that purpose. . . . The time has come when this land must be cultivated. White people will come here and cultivate it under any circumstances. No power on earth can prevent it."[35] Lieutenant-Governor Archibald also explained that, in his view, the Anishinabe did not have a right to this particular land, given that the Cree had inhabited the area first and moved west with the buffalo herds, roughly a century earlier, "and the Chippewa, finding the land unoccupied, came in and stopped here, but they have no rights to the land beyond that."[36]

Ayee-ta-pe-pe-tung challenged the commissioner: "You say the white man found this country, and that we were not the first Indians in it. What is the name of the first Indian found along the sea coast?"[37] The commissioner said he was "afraid some evil bird was whispering in Council. The Commissioner again showed the Indians that they were unwise in not closing with the terms offered."[38] The Anishinabe were again threatened with the prospect that "white men would come in and take up land, and that without the treaty the Indians would in the long run be left without any land to cultivate.[39] The Anishinabe had their own views about how the land was to be used.

The atmosphere had become tense, and it appeared that the Indians saw no benefit in making the treaty on the terms being offered (annuities and reserves). This was far less than what they already possessed.

Breakdown in Negotiations

After a two-hour break in the negotiations, Chief Kasias "came forward with an attendant gaily painted, wearing eagles' feathers, and something like a blue waterfall on top of his head."[40] In his view, he could not see how he would be enriched by what was being offered by the treaty.

Wa-sus-koo-koon and other chiefs came forward to shake hands and depart,

> and the invariable ceremony of shaking hands with His Excellency and the Commissioner having been gone through, the brave harangued the crowd, protesting that he could not live on ten shillings if he were to settle down. He also complained of the insufficiency of reserves. Look, he said, at the farmers with all their property; they spent a great deal of money before getting to be as they are. We want the reserve we have asked for and cannot take your terms.[41]

The Anishinabe treaty was, by all appearances, not going to be concluded.

Ayee-ta-pe-pe-tung said that he "would take a winter to think over the matter before entering into a treaty." McKay then "made an eloquent speech in Indian explaining matters."[42] There is no description of what he said, or whether it was ever translated for the Commissioner and Lieutenant-Governor. Whatever was said may have prompted Ayee-ta-pe-pe-tung to revise his position as a consequence, and to request more money, on behalf of his band of Indians. The commissioner again addressed the Indians and threatened to break up negotiations unless they came to a close the following day.

On the last day of negotiations, it was clear that the Indians' uncertainty with respect to the land question had not been attenuated. Henry Prince spoke of his confusion and the questions that remained. He recalled his father's dying words, requesting that he retain the land (possibly referring to the lands that were reserved exclusively for the Anishinabe in the Selkirk Treaty — everything outside the two-mile tracts of land along the rivers). "Again, I wish to say that nearly the last words my father said before dying were — There is the line — keep it; and we want to retain it."[43] In response, the Lieutenant-Governor made a lengthy statement "showing that the Queen was willing to help the Indians in every way [and] would give them a school and a school master for each reserve, and for those who desired to cultivate the soil, ploughs and harrows would be provided on the reserves."[44]

And yet, there was still no agreement on the terms of the treaty. Chief Wa-sus-koo-koon "insisted on having the reserve he had specified before."[45] Other Chiefs made speeches and "extravagant demands," which were reported in The Manitoban newspaper in the following way:

> A good deal of parley ensued, in the course of which the Indians made new and extravagant demands, while the Commissioner and His Excellency reasoned with them, and refused to give way any more. . . . Another meeting and more speechifying — the Indians continuing their extravagant demands as before.[46]

The chiefs had met and agreed in council on their approach to the negotiations (with the exception of the Indians from the Portage, as noted). They resisted the division that was being created among them by the commissioner and the Lieutenant-Governor. Henry Prince, Grand Oreilles, Kasias, and Wa-sus-koo-koon came forward. Wa-sus-koo-koon spoke on behalf of them and made known the views of the Indians (excluding those of the

Portage) and detailed lists of their wants, including fine clothes for the children in the spring and in the fall, furnished houses, ploughs, cattle, farm implements, buggies for the chiefs, and supplies for hunting, and other supplies as required:

> I am going to state the wants of all the Indians — not including those of the Portage. First, in the early part of every spring, we want all the children to be clothed with fine clothes! In the fall of the year they are to be clothed from head to foot with warm clothing! Whenever an Indian wants to settle, a house is to be put up for him fully furnished, and a plough, with all its accompaniments of cattle, etc. complete, is to be given him! We want buggies for the chiefs, councillors and braves, to show their dignity! Each man is to be supplied with whatever he sees for hunting, and all his other requirements, and the women in the same way!! Each Indian settling on the reserve is to be free from taxes! If you grant this request, continued the brave with utmost gravity, I will say you have shown kindness to me and to the Indians.[47]

The commissioner mocked the chiefs, saying that he would rather be an Indian if those were the terms agreed to:

> I am proud of being an Englishman. But if Indians are going to be dealt with in this way, I will take off my coat and change places with the speaker, for it would be far better to be an Indian. (This sally was too much even for Indian gravity, and there was a general roar of laughter in which Wa-sus-koo-koon himself joined in as heartily as any).[48]

While the record indicates that laughter followed, it does not indicate that the demands had been refused by the commissioner.[49]

An Unexplained Shift

The record of the negotiations at this point becomes very brief. There were other speeches that are not described, either in form or content. Before the end of the second-to-last day's proceedings, "the Portage chief and his followers left, formally bidding the Lieut.-Governor and the Commissioner goodbye."[50] The other bands were also prepared to leave the negotiations,

James McKay asked them to stay on one more night, "promising that in the interval he (McKay) would try and bring the Commissioner and the Indians closer together."[51] It is unclear what James McKay said or did during the evening, but the chiefs remained at the Fort and signed the treaty the following day, the eighth and final day of the negotiations. The treaty was signed, with no further terms negotiated, nor any explanation on the record of what had transpired to change the collective minds of the chiefs. The chiefs were "in better humour," and signed the treaty promptly:

> All the Indians met His Excellency and the Commissioner today in better humour. The Commissioner said he understood they were disposed to sign the treaty. . . . This gave general satisfaction, and the treaty was soon signed, sealed and delivered, with all due formality. The ceremony was witnessed by a large crowd of spectators.[52]

Conclusion

What was understood by the Anishinabe flowing from these negotiations? Many theories about the treaty have been espoused by historians, ethnohistorians, lawyers, and political scientists. Early analyses point to deceit and manipulation. Some claim that the Anishinabe did not understand western concepts of property law, which confused the concepts of "surrender" and "sharing" of land. At times, the Anishinabe have themselves remarked that the treaties "were and are unconscionable by virtue of the distortions, inequities, and the inconsistencies implicit in the negotiations."[53]

Refined analyses raise the possibilty of inept translation of words and concepts, which led to misunderstanding. Historians such as Jean Friesen[54] have found that, faced with a difficult situation, the Anishinabe made the best deal they could, and that they surrendered the land, but retained some jurisdiction over resources. While I agree with Friesen that the chiefs were in a sense forced to negotiate, I take a different view about the resulting agreement. The Anishinabe *inaakonigewin* (law) relating to land and the use of land informed the negotiations. Whether those laws were understood by the Crown cannot be confirmed; there are indications in the record that the Crown negotiators did have an understanding that the Anishinabe were not approaching land issues using an acquisition and possession model. It is my view, based on the evidence taken as a whole, that the Anishinabe agreed to share the land with the settlers and to allow them to use the land they desired for agriculture. The Anishinabe also understood that they could continue to use their territory for their traditional activities. Neither party would interfere with the other. On the question of reserves, lands would be kept separate and could be used by the Anishinabe, should they choose to farm. Neither traditional harvesting nor farming were mutually exclusive, the result being that the Anishinabe would continue to use the land of Treaty One, along with the settlers, in a spirit of equality and non-interference. This is what the elders refer to as a "sharing treaty."

Friesen points out that natural resources were not mentioned in Treaties One and Two, but were mentioned in all other numbered treaties, and in the Robinson and Douglas treaties. In her view, the Anishinabe drew a distinction between land and natural resources. She further argues that, once the continuing use of resources was confirmed in the opening speeches (what was to be retained), the discussion moved to what would be given. An alternative perspective, in which land and resources are captured under one concept — *Nimaamaa Aki* (Mother Earth), with whom the Anishinabe have a direct relationship — is reflective of the normative principles that were invoked in the treaty negotiations and which reflect ongoing normative values. Based on some Anishinabe understandings of the relationship with the land, the land itself has no value independent of its resources, which are placed on the land in order to be shared.

Use of resources in areas under the jurisdiction (or use) of another group would be requested:

> We had a basic understanding and belief that it was to be shared. I remember the many political discussions about that and about rice, wild rice and the harvesting of rice, and how in this area, we liked to believe that this was ours. And some elders from the back said, this is the Creator's garden. That's the Creator's garden. It doesn't belong to one tribe, it belongs to the ones that believe in the spirit of the gift that we call wild rice.[55]

It is possible then to conceive that Treaty One was understood by the Anishinabe not as a surrender of land, but as an agreement to share the land and its resources in the following way: plots of agricultural land for the White settlers and continued use of the land for harvesting by the Anishinabe. Elder Victor Courchene explains it in the following way:

The Anishinabe understood that they never gave up everything. They threw an axe in the soil and said "this is how much we will give up". . . . The Queen's representatives asked for only the top six inches of our land so that the white man could farm. They were only given this amount. That is the main thing. [56]

Elder Charlie Nelson explains that nothing was given up, that the Anishinabe only agreed to share the land:

We need the government to understand that we have been kind, we have been sharing. Now you need to hear some of that truth. We have not given up in our treaties the tree, the sweetgrass, the medicines from the sweetgrass, the animals, and the rock. . . . we have not given those in our treaty rights. The treaty right that was given to the people that came here was for them for agricultural purposes. So now you have agricultural purposes. [57]

Reserves would be set aside for the Indians, if and when they chose agriculture, although it was promised that they would never be compelled to farm. "The different bands will get such quantities of land as will be sufficient for their use in adopting the habits of the White man, should they choose to do so." [58] The settlers' use of land was explained as being generally limited to agriculture, as had been agreed to in the past with Selkirk, and as was explained in the opening statements to the Treaty One negotiations. When asked to clarify the concept of reserves, the Lieutenant-Governor explained, "reserves did not mean hunting grounds, but merely portions of land set aside to form a farm for each family. A large portion of the country would remain as much a hunting ground as ever after the Treaty closed." [59]

The treaty negotiations were muddled by two land concepts that were being canvassed concurrently: the surrender of land for the entire treaty area and the setting aside of reserves for the Indians, neither of which could be related to Anishinabe concepts of land tenure. The conceptual distinction between the surrender of the entirety of the land (which included the traditional territory of each of the bands present) and the reserves that would be set aside for Indian agriculture is a significant one. Although the concept of reserves of land set aside for the Indians was discussed at length, there is no conclusive indication on the record that the differing views were ever really reconciled.

From Commissioner Simpson's perspective, after the refusal of the chiefs' original reserve selections, the matter of reserves had been clarified. There is no detail on the record as to what was said or done, beyond showing the Indians diagrams of lots that they would acquire, in order to induce the Anishinabe to reduce their original reserve selection from roughly two thirds of the province to a much smaller selection which reflected the formula of 160 acres per family of five. The reserves were to be surveyed and allocated after the treaty and would reflect the land allocation based on the treaty annuity lists that would be developed.

It appears from the record and subsequent interactions between the Anishinabe and the Crown that the size of the reserves was likely not commonly agreed upon in the negotiations. As Hallowell notes, the Anishinabe generally measure distance in units of activity.[60] "As for land, what mattered most for the Ojibwe were the distribution and frequency of animal and plant resources on the land (and along the waterways); the measuring of areas in abstract spatial terms was not a useful or relevant exercise."[61]

The concept of what would be retained for exclusive use by the Anishinabe was improperly understood at the time of treaty, arguably by both parties. Today, the term "reserve" is translated by the Anishinabe word *ishkonigan*. This may have been used as a term to explain the concept of "reserve" at the treaty negotiations. Harry Bone, an Anishinabe elder, explains the concept of reserve as land that was set aside for ourselves, not "leftovers":

Ishkonigan does not mean "leftover" to us, ishkonigan means *gigii-mii-ishkonaamin* in other words "we left this land aside for ourselves" not leftover. Leftover is kind of a loose meaning and has a different connotation. For us, the Elders told us that, *gigii-mii-ishkonaamin* – meaning we left some part of that land for ourselves, that is what it means. *Gigii-mii-ishkonaamin* — in other words, here is the land, it's not left over and that is not what the intent was, set aside, we set aside for ourselves this land.[62]

Elder Bone's comments illustrate the incompatibility between the concepts that were put forward by the Crown and those relied on by the Anishinabe.

Assurances of continued use were made in relation to the whole of the land, whereas promises to set aside reserves for agricultural use were made for those who would want to shift to an agricultural lifestyle (although the

Queen promised not to force the Indians to farm). From the Anishinabe perspective, the land relationship being proposed was one by which they would continue to use the land for their traditional activities of hunting, trapping, fishing, and harvesting, with shared use by the settlers for agricultural purposes, and with a promise to have selected lands set aside for their farms, should they choose to engage in agriculture. This was in keeping with Anishinabe *inaakonigewin* related to land, which allowed for and encouraged shared use of land for sustenance and non-interference with another's use of land for a specific purpose:

> A spirit of mutual helpfulness is manifest in the sharing of economic goods and there is every evidence of cooperation in all sorts of economically productive tasks. No one, in fact, is much better off than his neighbour. Dependence upon hunting, fishing, and trapping for a living is precarious at best and it is impossible to accumulate food for the inevitable rainy day. If I have more than I need I share it with you today because I know that you, in turn, will share your surplus with me tomorrow.[63]

From the record of the negotiations, it is clear that the Anishinabe were hesitant throughout the negotiations about the extent to which the treaty would modify their relationship to the land. They were concerned about the continued use of the land, as well as their relationship with incoming settlers. Concern was expressed for the well-being of the land itself and for future generations:

> When they signed the Treaty they didn't want anything for themselves, it was for the future generations. It was for the children. Seven generations was what they looked at, this is the Anishinabe teaching.[64]

It is fundamentally problematic that the concepts of surrender and extinguishment of title were never raised or discussed at the negotiations. Had they been, they would likely have resulted in an immediate breakdown in the negotiations, as the Anishinabe would not have agreed to a surrender of the land. In addition, the use of particular words in both the Anishinabe language and the English language at the treaty negotiations were infused with particular legal meaning. For example, English vocabulary relating to property was infused with common law content. The Royal Commission on Aboriginal Peoples report confirmed that "terms such as cede, surrender, extinguish, yield and forever give up all rights and titles appear in the written text of the treaties, but discussion of the meaning of these concepts is not found anywhere in the records of treaty negotiations."[65] The Anishinabe perspective on lands, the lawful obligations that they had toward the land, and obligations to share with others in the bounty of the land cannot be translated into common law property concepts. Even if the Anishinabe had a vague understanding of British or Canadian concepts of ownership, they likely did not perceive themselves as being bound by them. Similarly, the settlers likely did not view themselves as bound by Anishinabe laws, with the possible exception of some of their earlier trade or political interactions with the Anishinabe, such as those illustrated in previous chapters.

Building on Stone Foundations:

Relationships and Protocols[1]

Concept of law (handwritten margin note)

In relying on Anishinabe laws as a way of understanding treaty, we must first consider how we understand law itself. What is meant by the term "law"? "Where do we stop speaking of law and find ourselves simply describing social life?"[2] Gordon Woodman suggests that "law covers a continuum which runs from the clearest form of state law through to the vaguest forms of informal social control."[3] Can we distinguish between customs and "laws" (as conceived by positivists)? Or do we accept, like Lon Fuller, that all law is customary (including statutes) and "owes its force to the fact that it has found direct expression in the conduct of men toward one another."[4] Webber finds that "[t]o understand law is to understand norms' relationship to the web of human interaction in a given society."[5]

The individual, outside of the social and collective, is incapable of creating law: it is necessarily interactive and culturally rooted. Although there isn't one uniform view of law among the Anishinabe, Anishinabe *inaakonigewin* (law) is generally found to be all about relationships. For the purposes of this work, I will not focus on sharp distinctions between formal and informal systems of law, but will consider all forms of normative ordering.

In addition, because of the prevailing notion that Indigenous laws are contained in language, I work from the understanding that language itself (including translations) affects understandings and legal commitments.[6] Cultural, social, and linguistic perspectives are critical to the analysis of the Treaty One negotiations. They help illustrate the application of different legal systems, the overlap between them and the potential variations in terms of the legal significance of some of the elements of the treaty negotiations.

Recognition of Indigenous Legal Traditions

Indigenous legal systems are profoundly complex and consist of multiple sources. According to John Borrows, law consists of "formal and informal elements. It pivots around deeply complex explicit and implicit ideas and practices related to respect, order and authority. Laws arise whenever inter-personal interactions create expectations and obligations about proper conduct."[7] Borrows lists the following sources of Indigenous law: sacred, natural, deliberative, positivistic, and customary.

But how should Indigenous legal traditions interact with other legal traditions within Canada? Although Indigenous legal traditions have been recognized by the Supreme Court of Canada, challenges arise as to how to value, understand, and respect Indigenous laws, along with questions of whether this recognition should take place within the Canadian legal system. In Borrows' view, Canada has three legal traditions: common law, civil law, and Indigenous law, although he acknowledges that this is not a universally held view:

> There is a debate about what constitutes "law" and whether Indigenous peoples in Canada practiced law prior to European arrival. Some contemporary commentators have said that Indigenous peoples in North America were pre-legal. Those who take this view believe that societies only possess laws if they are declared by some recognized power that is capable of enforcing such a proclamation. They may argue that Indigenous tradition is only customary, and therefore not clothed with legality.[8]

Borrows argues that Indigenous legal systems pre-date British or Canadian law and continue to co-exist with (or exist alongside) Canadian law.[9] "Put simply, Canada's Aboriginal peoples were here when Europeans came, and were never conquered."[10] Brian Slattery,[11] James (Sa'ke'j) Youngblood Henderson[12] and Borrows argue that "when treaties are made they can be seen as creating an inter-societal framework in which first laws intermingle with Imperial laws to foster peace and order across communities."[13]

Within the academic study of law, there is a project, championed by John Borrows, Jeremy Webber, Val Napoleon[14] and others, which seeks to recognize and promote Indigenous legal traditions. In some ways this work differs from modern understandings and applications of Indigenous laws and considerations about their place within the Canadian constitutional framework. I place importance on understanding the articulation of an Indigenous legal tradition as it existed at the time of the Treaty One negotiations, when two parallel and autonomous systems of law coexisted within one geographical space at one particular time, namely the Province of Manitoba[15] in 1871. While the British common law applied to White subjects of the Crown that were in the territory, the Anishinabe were governed by their own legal tradition. Some exceptions might have arisen when individual Anishinabe entered into valid contracts with fur trade companies.

My focus is less on the inter-societal framework[16] that may have been achieved through the treaties or the continued and modern existence of our Indigenous laws, but rather on the independent understandings that gave rise to and formed the foundations of the treaties. Attempting to explore the different and differing legal principles that applied to treaty making may help us better understand the expectations that flowed from the treaties.[17] Although I accept that, to some extent, Indigenous and non-Indigenous societies had begun to engage in a "*modus vivendi* that became the foundation of a normative community that crossed the cultural divide,"[18] this engagement was, at best, in its infancy at the time Treaty One was negotiated, primarily because the foundations of that normative community to date had relied so extensively on Anishinabe protocols and normative principles of interaction, such as kinship. The systems of normative understanding of the Anishinabe remained largely independent of those of the settlers and Crown.

Multiple Systems of Law

Prior to the negotiation of Treaty One, Anishinabe *inaakonigewin* existed alongside and, in some cases, in complex systems of interaction with other legal traditions. As illustrated in Chapter One, the Anishinabe fostered long-standing legal relationships with other Indigenous nations in relation to lands and treaty making. In addition, during the seventeenth and eighteenth centuries, the relationship between the Anishinabe of Treaty One and the fur traders[19] was characterized primarily by the adoption of Anishinabe *inaakonigewin* into the "commercial compacts" that were concluded between the trading parties.[20] Outside the context of trade interactions, non-Indigenous laws law applied to White traders, while *inaakonigewin* continued to apply to the Anishinabe. "The Aboriginal peoples' and the colonist's own normative orders did not disappear in this new community. They retained their specificity. . . ."[21]

To understand how Treaty One may have been informed by the Anishinabe legal perspective, one must begin with the premises that multiple legal traditions can exist in one geographic space at one time, and that, while at some level they interact, they exist independently of one another. In this case, by considering the non-hierarchical co-existence of two distinct and autonomous legal systems (Anishinabe and western),[22] in what is now Manitoba, at the time of making Treaty One, we can better understand the importance of examining the treaty from the perspectives of both legal cultures.[23]

Put simply, Anishinabe *inaakonigewin* co-existed with other systems of law at the time of Treaty One negotiations and therefore should be considered in order to better understand and interpret the treaty.

Anishinabe *inaakonigewin* and Treaty

Borrows relates that "Anishinabek law was all about relationships."[24] It is not codified, but is taught. Anishinabe *inaakonigewin* and teachings are also learned directly from the Earth and other beings, "from the plants, insects, birds, animals, the daily changes in the weather, the motion of the wind and the waters, and the complexion of the stars, the moon and the sun. They didn't write these down but kept them in their hearts."[25] Laws are also infused and contained in the *Anishinabemowin* language and passed down through the teachings related to *mino-bimaadiziwin* (leading a good life):

> [T]he Ojibway worldview is expressed through their language and through the Law of the Orders, which instructs people about the right way to live. The standards of conduct which arise from the Law of the Orders are not codified, but are understood and passed on from generation to generation. Correct conduct is concerned with "appropriate behaviour, what is forbidden, and the responsibility ensuing from each." The laws include relationships among human beings as well as the correct relationship with other orders: plants, animals and the physical world. The laws are taught through "legends" and other oral traditions.[26]

Much of Anishinabe *inaakonigewin* is related to kinship and land.[27] Legal relationships exist between various animate beings.[28] These relationships exist among humans, animals, fish, plants, rocks, and *adisookan* (spirits), among and between themselves individually and collectively. Treaties were made between the Anishinabe and the Animal Nations.[29] These relationships are described in terms of kinship, the trees and rocks being our brothers, "meaning those who knew more and were stronger."[30] The sun and moon are our grandfather and grandmother, the earth our mother. Each depends on the other, the Anishinabe being most dependent of all on their relations:

> Our ancestors saw a kinship between plants, insects, birds, animals, fish and human beings, a kinship of dependence; humans depending on animals and birds and insects; animals depending on insects and plants; insects depending on plants; plants depending only on the earth, sun, and rain. Creation was conducted in a certain order: plants, insects, birds, animals and human beings. In the order of necessity, humans were the last and the least; they would not last long without the other forms of beings.[31]

The Anishinabe define their obligations and responsibilities in terms of their relationships. According to Anishinabe elder Harry Bone, the first of these relationships is between the Anishinabe and the Creator.[32] The second is between the Anishinabe and *Nimaamaa Aki* (Mother Earth). Borrows finds that as Anishinabe we "can't properly exercise our agency or make the best choices without remembering the land."[33] These are followed by relationships between the air, wind, fire, animals, plants, birds, and fish. These relationships exist between all things at all times.

While some anthropologists and social scientists have used the term "fictive kinship" to describe relationships that are created between individuals who are not biologically related, this does not begin to capture kinship relationships as defined in Anishinabe *inaakonigewin*. There is no fiction in Anishinabe kinship. The Anishinabe are kin to the rocks, the trees, the animals, the birds, the fish, to each other, and to "the other." "The Saulteaux kinship system is centripal in tendency in the sense that everyone with whom one comes in social contact not only falls within the category of a relative, but a blood relative, through the extension in usage of a few primary terms."[34]

Each relationship carries with it responsibilities and obligations. These are generally mutual obligations, although less importance is placed on equal and immediate return within a relationship. While Jean Friesen[35] and others consider "balanced reciprocity" (an equal and specified return) to be the guiding principle of relationships, in Anishinabe *inaakonigewin*, reciprocity is more of a general nature, with the possibility of return at a future or unknown date and of an undetermined value. Hallowell argues that, for the Northern Ojibway, "[i]t is within this web of social relations that the individual strives for *pimadiziwin*,"[36] a good life.[37]

When we consider the terms of Anishinabe *inaakonigewin* in this way, the relationships and the obligations that accompany them become the defining feature of the relationship, rather than the emphasis being placed on the source of the relationship. Relationships thus define the *roles* of each living thing in this creation. In turn, the obligations and responsibilities come from our role in creation. "To our ancestors it was self evident that all creatures were born equal and free to come and go and fulfill their purposes as intended by Kitchi-Manitou."[38]

Building on Solid Foundations: Relationships and Protocols

Since creation,[39] *inaakonigewin* applied to the Anishinabe. As discussed earlier, Anishinabe *inaakonigewin* was also applied jointly with other Indigenous legal traditions in order to secure peace, alliance, and trade among Indigenous nations. Also, in the early years of contact between the Europeans and the Anishinabe prior to Treaty One, Anishinabe *inaakonigewin* applied in some interactions with Europeans: for example, in fur trade relations. Relationships that developed between the Anishinabe and the French and British Crowns were heavily informed by Anishinabe practices and protocols.

The mutual reliance of the treaty parties on Anishinabe protocols, or procedural law, invoked substantive normative expectations on the part of the Anishinabe, which informed the development of the Treaty One relationship. Although the use of procedural law may not have been completely understood by the treaty negotiators, they adopted the protocols for the purposes of securing the treaty. Janna Promislow argues that, similarly, in the context of the fur trade, the "protocol acquired a normative dimension for HBC traders because it was how things were done, not because it was understood or respected."[40]

In the discussion that follows, I outline some clear examples of the protocols or procedural norms employed in the Treaty One negotiations, which invoke elements of substantive Anishinabe laws, including expectations involving the normative obligations associated with particular relationships. The procedural norms that are detailed below include waiting for all to be present before beginning the proceedings, speaking only when authorized by the people to do so, removing obstructions to good communication and negotiation, gifting and feasting the treaty partners, and adhering to ceremonial protocol.

The focus of this discussion is not on whether the application or extent of those laws was known or understood by the Crown representatives. Rather, the point is that the Crown's invocation and adherence to those protocols almost certainly informed the Anishinabe understanding of the obligations resulting from the product of these negotiations, given their normative and historical significance within the Anishinabe legal culture of the time.

Relationships between Groups — Waiting for the Others, Authority to Speak

Although the Treaty One negotiations were set to begin on July 25, 1871, they were delayed for two days due to the late arrival of some of the bands. While some preliminary discussions took place, those Anishinabe who were present would not agree to start the negotiations without the other bands. "On the part of the Indians, it was stated that they were not ready to open a Treaty, as a large number of the tribes — those from the upper country — were not present."[41] These protocols were recognized and accepted by the commissioners as necessary to the negotiation process, as they agreed to wait two days for the others to arrive, all the while feeding those who had assembled. Once all of the bands were represented, the negotiations began.[42]

Commissioner Simpson equated the delay in negotiations with what he perceived as jealousy between the bands in relation to their communication with the Crown:

Amongst them, as amongst other Indians with whom I have come in contact, there exists great jealousy of one another, in all matters relating to their communications with the officials of Her Majesty and in order to facilitate the object in view, it was most desirable that suspicion and jealousy of all kinds should be allayed.[43]

Although jealousy may have existed amongst the bands,[44] a more robust understanding of this protocol suggests that the Anishinabe who first arrived at the Stone Fort respected the autonomy of each band and adhered to principles of non-interference in each other's affairs. Henry Prince explained that when he did things, he did them for the benefit of all Indians, although he acknowledged the limits of his jurisdiction by explaining that his authority extended only "as far as Fort Garry," the geographical boundary of his band's territory:

> Whatever I do, I do it for all the Indians. I have done it always for all the Indians ever since my father spoke for them (at Lord Selkirk's treaty). When I want to speak about my father I speak loud, and am always glad to speak about him, but whenever I get to say anything, my voice only goes as far as Fort Garry.[45]

At the outset of the negotiations, the chiefs were selected to speak on behalf of their bands. One band or chief could not speak for another band without their express permission. Where they spoke for another individual or for a group, the indicated this clearly. For example, "Henry Prince said that

A depiction of the Treaty One negotiations held at Lower Fort Garry, summer 1871. Archives of Manitoba, Events 243/1 (N11975).

he could not then enter upon any negotiations, as he was not empowered to speak or act for those bands of Indians not then present."[46] The Anishinabe were offered *asemaa* (tobacco) and deliberated on the issue of who their speakers would be. Although the speakers were to deliver messages on behalf of the people, they did not make decisions on behalf of the others, they simply relayed the views of their people. When one of the chiefs at the negotiations stated that the Anishinabe would enter into the treaty if the annuity were increased, he was immediately corrected by the other chiefs, as he had not consulted with them and could not speak on their behalf. He then clarified that "he only spoke for his own camp fire."[47] This non-interference is illustrative of a respect for the internal jurisdiction of each band over its affairs.

There was also a degree of individual autonomy and agency in collective decision making. Decisions were made by consulting with individuals. For example, reserves were selected collectively: "the Indians themselves are always consulted as to where they will want it — whether all in one place, or in several."[48] There was a profound sense of equality between all members of a band: "[t]he Anishinaubaek came and went as they pleased, with-out having to ask permission of the chief or some master. Men and women stood, sat, talked, walked, and worked with chiefs and leaders. They were equal."[49] Where there was disagreement with the general direction of a band, people were free to remove themselves from the collective. When decisions had to be made which would have an impact beyond the band, the chiefs of the various bands met in council:

> [T]hey are shrewd and sufficiently awake to their own interests, and, if the matter should be one of importance, affecting the general interests of the tribe, they neither reply to a proposition, nor make one themselves, until it is fully discussed and deliberated upon in Council by all the Chiefs. . . .[50]

During the negotiations, when asked whether they wanted reserves in one place or several, Chief Kasias responded that the "chiefs must consult with each other and would reply next morning."[51]

Thus, the Treaty One negotiations were founded on protocols of waiting for others and not speaking for others without proper authority. These protocols illustrate the reliance on substantive principles of non-interference and respect for the autonomous jurisdiction of smaller collectives, and individuals.

Relationships to other Anishinabe — *Removing the Dark Cloud*

Once the commissioners had made their opening remarks, the second day of negotiations commenced with an expression of discontentment that shadowed the negotiations. The Anishinabe expressed that "[t]here was a cloud before them which made things dark, and they did not wish to commence the proceedings till the cloud was dispersed."[52] They explained that four Anishinabe men had been imprisoned, for allegedly failing to have fulfilled their terms of employment with the HBC. They were imprisoned at the Fort. The chiefs asked that the prisoners be released prior to the negotiations. The Lieutenant-Governor, pushing back against this strong assertion, released the prisoners "as a matter of favour, not as a matter of right,"[53] but not without first confirming that the Anishinabe did not disregard "White law." The Lieutenant-Governor asked the Indians if they "were under the impression that they were liable to the law"[54] and stated that all men, whether White or Indian would be punished in the same way for breaches of the law (presumably British law as applied in Manitoba):

> I stated that the Queen knew no distinction between her subjects. If a man does wrong, whether white man or an Indian, he had to suffer for it. If a white man makes a bargain with an Indian and does not fulfil it, the Queen will punish the white man. If, on the other hand, an Indian does wrong to an Indian or white man, the law is the same; he will be punished. I wish you to understand that all men, whether white or Indian, must obey the law.[55]

Chief Ayee-ta-pe-pe-tung explained that although he did not wish to disregard the law that had provided for the imprisonment of the men, the obstacle that their imprisonment created had to be cleared away in order for the parties to work toward a treaty:

> I can scarcely hear the Queen's words. An obstacle is in the way. Some of my children are in that building (pointing to the jail). That is the obstacle in the way which prevents me responding to the Queen's words. I am not fighting against law and order; but I want my young men to be free, and then I will be able to answer. I hold my own very sacred, and therefore, could not work while my child is sitting in the dark. [...]

We are going to make a treaty with the Queen, and want to clean everything away from the ground that it may be clean. We are going to work and will work better if every obstacle is cleared away. I am not defying the law, but would wish to have the Saulteaux at present in jail, liberated.[56]

The prisoners were released, allowing the negotiations to proceed. When the prisoners were ordered released, "the sky became clear."[57] Although Archibald stated that he was releasing the four men as a favour, on behalf of the Queen,[58] the result was that there was an adherence to the Anishinabe protocol of starting things "in a good way," with no ill feeling toward the others. This action demonstrates respect for the Anishinabe treaty negotiators and whether it was meant to be or not, a recognition of Anishinabe jurisdiction over their own people.

Just months before the Treaty negotiations, in May 1871, seventy-three "Principal Indians" of Portage La Prairie (including Chief Yellow Quill and Iei-te-pee-tung — possibly Ayee-ta-pe-pe-tung who negotiated Treaty One) had issued resolutions in council protesting the behaviour of the settlers. In particular, they decried the way "they come about searching our tents, and carrying away our people to other lands, when we think they have no business with us at all." [59] They resolved that if their people were taken away, they would require a payment of five pounds sterling, one pound for every day they were detained thereafter, or five pounds for every day they would spend in jail. They communicated their resolutions to the Lieutenant-Governor in writing immediately, reminding him that he had promised to make treaty with them that spring.

It is worth noting that the discussion in relation to the application of British law to the Indians may not have been similarly understood by each of the parties. While *The Manitoban* report indicates that Ayee-ta-pe-pe-tung "made a predatory flourish about Indian lands, and then came to the point . . . ," it is uncertain as to what can be taken from the chief's words.

An important part of the context in which the detainment of the men in this particular circumstance can be understood is that it involved a breach of contractual obligations between the HBC and its employees, who happened to be Indians. Although the Lieutenant-Governor was seeking confirmation that the Indians had due regard for Crown law (presumably British law, as it was being applied in Manitoba), it could be inferred that the affirmation by Chief Ayee-ta-pe-pe-tung was limited to situations in which

Indians agreed to enter into a relationship where they would subject themselves to British law (i.e., on entering into contractual relationships with the HBC). Again, there is room for nuance in this discussion.

Similarly, in the context of Treaty Nine discussions, Long finds that Anishinabe concepts of law differed from Euro-Canadian concepts, although these distinctions may not have been fully understood at the time of treaty:

> It is highly unlikely that the Ojibwe and Cree understood the Euro-Canadian concept of "law." The closest Ojibwe word, *onaakonigewin*, referred to a plan or decision. . . . Most of their own laws were values about sharing, cooperation, and other culturally proper behaviours so essential to their survival and well-being — literally, the laws of the land. . . . These decisions, or laws, were necessary for maintaining *bimaadiziwin*. . . .[60]

Once again, the issue of jurisdiction over Anishinabe people was put squarely on the treaty table, by requesting the release of the prisoners. Nonetheless, one can see how the resolution of the matter may have had varying significance for each of the parties.

Relationships with Guests — Gifting and Feasting

It is customary for the Anishinabe to give *asemaa* (tobacco) and gifts to secure relationships or when asking something of another. Bruce White notes that gifts "aided in establishing and affirming more elaborate relationships. Depending on the situations in which they were given and on the words and ceremonies that accompanied them, gifts communicated something."[61] The political and spiritual worlds of the Anishinabe were connected to one another, and were rooted in relations of kinship in which reciprocal obligations of care were continuously reaffirmed through gift-giving. "Peaceful relations with the surrounding elements of the natural world and peoples within that world meant establishing and maintaining relationships of spiritual kinship by creating reciprocal obligations of care. To give or receive presents was to renounce the status of alien and to become kin."[62]

As had been the practice of the Hudson's Bay Company over the years, and of the Crown in past treaty negotiations with the Anishinabe, gifts were presented at the Treaty One negotiations. Chief Ayee-ta-pe-pe-tung explained that when "the President of the United States authorizes a man to come and treat with Indians, he brings with him heaps of goods to give over to them as a present."[63] The Anishinabe demanded the same of the commissioner who had invited them to the treaty negotiations. "It is not the wish of our Great Mother that her children should be fed on more than one kind of provision? Is it her wish that this day her children should go to the hunting ground to bring in fresh meat?"[64] A "sly old brave" told a story of proper hosting, which was a clear indication about how the Anishinabe expected to be treated in the negotiations — as they had been in the past — with provisions for the duration of the negotiations. [65]

The Crown representatives fed those assembled, recognizing that if they did not, they would likely leave to hunt and gather. Simpson was prepared to incur significant expense to secure the treaty: "I fear we shall have to incur a considerable expenditure for presents of food, etc., during the negotiations; but any cost for that purpose I shall deem a matter of minor consequence."[66]

Adherence to the protocol of feasting one's guests has a deep resonance with the Anishinabe. It entailed a respect for the Anishinabe who had been invited to the negotiations, and confirmed the obligations that the Crown had in hosting the negotiations and in future years. It confirmed that there was a relationship with the Crown and that the negotiations were being taken seriously.

As in past treaty relationships, including at the Selkirk Treaty,[67] the chiefs were presented with medals at the Treaty One negotiations.[68] In past treaty negotiations, medals had distributed by the British, French, Spanish, and the United States as signs of "friendship, allegiance and loyalty"[69] and to secure military, trade, or other treaty alliance. Renewal of obligations and relationships was significant to the Anishinabe, and past treaties had generally been founded on those principles. At Treaty One, the Crown proposed payment in the form of annuities (unlike the lump sum payments in the U.S.). While the annual payments may have been intended by the Anishinabe as an opportunity to renew the terms of the relationship, their intentions were possibly misapprehended. The Selkirk Treaty, which had been negotiated with the Anishinabe of the area 50 years earlier, had been negotiated on the basis of an annual payment of *asemaa* (tobacco) and was understood by the Anishinabe as a renewable lease of land.[70] While the Anishinabe may have expected a confirmation of the relationship and annual discussions about the ongoing terms of the agreement, the Crown approached the treaty as a one-time negotiation. "All the collateral expenses, therefore, of this year, including dresses, medals, presents to the Indians, etc., etc., will not appear in the expenses attending during future payments."[71] The Anishinabe might have expected that the feasting and gifting would be repeated annually, as was the case with the annual renewal of relationships between Indigenous nations, with the fur traders, and with the gifts that *Nimaamaa Aki* (Mother Earth) provided annually from her bounty.

Relationship with the Creator and Spirit — The Pipe

While waiting for the other bands to arrive on the first and second day of the treaty negotiations, an opening ceremony was conducted with dancing and drumming, to call on the spirit to guide the proceedings and to establish the parameters of the negotiations:

> The performances, between ribbons, feathers, paint and clothing, exhibited all the colors of the rainbow. There were two orchestras, half women and half men, one set playing for one style of dancing, and the other for another and very different one. The Band and performers were all seated on the grass, and the Commissioner, Lieut.-Governor and party, and a great crowd formed the spectators. Some of the chiefs and braves were in the most fashionable of dress — that is, dressed as little as possible; having merely breechclouts on; others had buffalo horns, etc., on their heads, while bears' claws, and similar rememberances [sic] were plentifully scattered through the group.[72]

The dance was also meant as an introduction to the parties, explaining the role and reputation of the chiefs and braves in accordance with Anishinabe custom and protocol.

Anishinabe Elders have related that the Treaty One negotiations were conducted in ceremony and that the spirit was called upon to assist the Anishinabe in the negotiations and in their decision making about their future and that of their grandchildren. Although the contemporaneous written record does not contain an explicit reference to a pipe ceremony, Simpson acknowledged the importance of the pipe and *asemaa* to the Anishinabe, particularly in relation to decision making. When Simpson asked the Anishinabe to select their spokesmen or representatives of the tribe, he "promised to send some tobacco to the camp, so that they might smoke over this matter and arrive at a decision that evening."[73]

The pipe and the pipe ceremony are sacred to the Anishinabe. The pipe ceremony is conducted to ensure peaceful dealings and to secure friendship among people or between the Anishinabe and the Creator.[74] In the pipe ceremony, the first whiff of smoke is offered in thanksgiving to the Creator.[75] The second is offered to *Nimaamaa Aki*. "The offerings of smoke were expressions of honour, respect, love, gratitude."[76] The pipe ceremony acknowledges the teachings and laws of the Anishinabe. The pipe brings unity into the gathering:

> The knowledge shared by the Elders tell [sic] us about the Creator's laws and sacred teachings. In the seven principles, the first belief is that there is only one Creator; the second belief is that we have a sacred spe-

Another depiction of the Treaty One negotiations held at Lower Fort Garry, summer 1871. Archives of Manitoba, Events 243/2 (N13290).

cial relationship with the land; the third belief is that we are all human people; the fourth belief is that we have a language; the fifth belief is that we have our culture and traditions through ceremonies; the sixth belief is that we have a history; and the seventh belief is that we are able to look after ourselves through our own forms of government. What this means is that the pipe is pointed in the seven directions during ceremony — to the Creator, to the land, to the people, and the four directions as represented by our languages, cultures, history and government. Each of these directions also have [sic] a specific teaching.[77]

Treaty One elders have confirmed that the treaty negotiations were conducted in ceremony and that the pipes were an important part of making the treaty. The pipe was used to call upon the Creator to act as a third party to the negotiations and the agreement. The Anishinabe would not have entered into such important negotiations without relying on the pipe to provide guidance and connection to the spirit. Charlie Nelson, a Treaty One Elder, referred to Treaty One as "a gathering of spirit." By invoking spirit, a solemn pledge to uphold any of the commitments made would have been confirmed. Some elders have told me that the treaty was "signed with the pipe." What I understand this to mean is that the treaty was confirmed by agreeing with the Creator to enter into a relationship with the Queen for shared use of the land.

When one accepts that the treaty agreement and promises were made with the Creator as a third party, the treaty cannot be breached. As with other Indigenous peoples, the Anishinabe view the treaty relationship as sacred.[78] "A treaty sanctified by the smoking of the pipe of peace became, in essence, a sacred text, a narrative that committed two different peoples to live according to a shared legal tradition — an American Indian vision of law and peace."[79] In order to ensure the proper adherence to the sacred promises, individuals were charged with the responsibility of remembering every detail of what was agreed to.

Ken Courchene, another Treaty One elder, speaks of the importance of *Gi-giigidowin* — keeping a promise, and the sacredness of promises. In Courchene's view, the treaty is a sacred promise that was made with the Creator and cannot be taken back:

Owe niiwin, the fourth one. *Gi-giigidowin* [your word, promise or vow]. *Giishin gegoo ashodaman* [If you make a promise] your word sacred. *Gishtwaa*. It means sacred. Your word is sacred. And a promise is a promise. You can't take it back. And a Treaty is that. That's a promise that they made not only to themselves but also to the Creator. That we would keep this as long as the sun shines, the earth is green and the waters flow. *Gi-gii-ganawendaamin* [We kept it — we keep it]. *Gaawiin gi-gii-biigwananziimin* [We did not break it]. We keep it. We didn't break that. Those words are sacred. It was a promise that we, owe *gi-gii-izhi-ganawaabamaanaaning gi-gii-zhi-misidotamaamin* [that we looked at them that way, that way I understood it]. . . . I want to believe that we were fair and honourable when our people sat before the Creator on mother earth and the people across from them would be as fair as they were. And those side deals and side promises, they took them to heart because they believed in them. So, it's very very important.[80]

Although the opening ceremony, the pipe, the Creator, and the involvement of spirit are not easily explained without reference to sacred *inaakonigewin*, adherence to these protocols helps to understand the approach that the Anishinabe take to the sacredness of treaty. This is the foundation for the Anishinabe assertion that the treaty cannot be "thrown out" or reneged on.

Conclusion

Adherence to Anishinabe protocols can be seen to have invoked substantive expectations and obligations from the Anishinabe perspective. From ceremonial and behavioural protocols, such as waiting for all of the parties to arrive, sitting together in a circle, releasing prisoners, feasting, offering *asemaa* and smoking the pipe, substantive principles of Anishinabe *inaakonigewin* became part of the treaty negotiations:

While European treaties borrowed the form of business contracts, Aboriginal treaties were modeled on the forms of marriage, adoption and kinship. They were aimed at creating living relationships and, like a marriage, they required periodic celebration, renewal, and reconciliation. . . . they were intended to grow and flourish as broad, dynamic relationships, changing and growing with the parties in a context of mutual respect and shared responsibility.[81]

Although the Crown negotiators may not have understood the full nuances of the norms that were invoked by the Anishinabe in the negotiations, they did rely on them, to a certain extent, to secure the treaty. As in the context of the fur trade, the treaty relationship may be one of those "relations in which divergent meanings were, perhaps, a defining characteristic."[82]

While the Crown may not have understood the full impact of the procedural laws of the Anishinabe, the fact remains that, to some extent, the treaty negotiators either relied on or allowed negotiations to be carried out in accordance with those principles. The reliance on these procedural principles of Anishinabe *inaakonigewin* invoked substantive legal principles and likely informed the Anishinabe understanding of what was being negotiated.

The Anishinabe approached treaty in accordance with their normative obligations of non-interference in each other's affairs, respect for each other's territories and jurisdiction, and commitment to the sacred nature of agreements made in ceremony. Procedural laws relating to respect for jurisdiction, non-interference, creation of kinship ties, feasting, dancing, and ceremony engaged a system of Anishinabe values and principles that had resonance in the agreement arrived at in treaty, including relationship, renewal, responsibility, and reciprocity. Legal principles of respect for autonomy and jurisdiction permeated the treaty relationships between the Anishinabe and the Crown, between groups of Anishinabe, among the Anishinabe as individuals, and in their relationship with the spirit.

Although the full extent of these substantive obligations may not have been fully understood by the Crown negotiators, and some of the norms may have been employed exploitatively, it remains the case that, by invoking them, the Anishinabe normative obligations were infused into the treaty relationship.

PART 3

ANISHINABE INAAKONIGEWIN

CHAPTER FIVE

Gizhagiiwin:

The Queen's Obligations of Love, Caring, Kindness, and Equality among her Children

Both the Crown and the Anishinabe relied heavily on the Queen acting as a mother to the Anishinabe and treating all her children equally. While the Commissioner and Lieutenant-Governor used the term mother more as a matter of form, knowing that the Anishinabe viewed their relationships in terms of kinship, the Anishinabe invoked the relationship to express its deeper implications and normative expectations, including long-term and inviolable commitments to preserving the welfare of their children. Drawing on the relationship of the Anishinabe with their primary mother figure, *Nimaamaa Aki*, Mother Earth, the Anishinabe chiefs and spokesmen illustrated the special bond and obligations of kindness, caring, and unconditional love, and of the earth's bounty, which ensured that the mother would care for the Anishinabe's needs.

Kinship with the Queen

Although in 1871, at the time of the treaty negotiations, Canada would have been the instructing authority with regard to treaties in western Canada, the written record of the negotiations, including the speeches by Lieutenant-Governor Archibald and Treaty Commissioner Simpson, and the written text of the treaty itself, refer only to the Queen and never to Canada. Henderson argues that a special relationship was formed between the Queen and the Anishinabe in the western treaties or "Victorian treaties."

"These treaties unified the Ojibwa Confederacy into an imperial relation-ship with the British Sovereign, distinct from either the United Kingdom or federal Parliamentary control."[1]

Much reference was made to the Queen in kinship terms, as a relative, the "Great Mother," by both the Crown representatives and the Anishinabe. At the Treaty One negotiations, both the commissioners and the Anishi-nabe referred extensively to the Queen as "mother" to the Anishinabe.

> Your Great Mother cannot come here herself to talk with you, but she has sent a messenger who has her confidence. Mr. Simpson will tell you truly all her wishes. . . .
>
> If you have any questions to ask, ask them, if you have anything you wish the Queen to know, speak out plainly. . . .
>
> When you hear his voice you are listening to your Great Mother the Queen, whom God bless and preserve long to reign over us.[2]

When Archibald opened the negotiations, he expressed to the Anishinabe that their mother was pleased with their behaviour the previous year, in particular, with the fact that they had not participated in the Red River Resistance. Their good conduct was referred to in the text of the treaty:

> With a view to show the satisfaction of Her Majesty with the behav-iour and good conduct of Her Indians . . . makes them a present of three dollars for each Indian man, woman and child belonging to the bands here represented.[3]

Archibald then introduced Simpson as the "chief" who would act on be-half of the Queen. Archibald stated that when Commissioner Simpson was speaking, the Anishinabe would be listening to the Queen: "when you hear his voice, you are listening to your Great Mother the Queen."[4] And the chiefs agreed: "in hearing the Commissioner this evening, I feel that we have heard the Queen's voice."[5] This relationship of kinship with the Queen is what secured the attendance and participation in the negotiations. Chief Sheeship was thankful to hear a message from his mother:

> I am thankful today that I have heard a message from our Great Mother, the Queen. The reason I got up from my seat was to come here and hear her voice. I am glad I have heard good tidings from

my mother; and if I live till tomorrow, I will send a requisition to her, begging her to grant me wherewith to make my living.[6]

The purpose of the meeting at the Stone Fort was explained in terms of a discussion relating to matters of interest to both parties. They were "to deliberate upon certain matters of interest to Her Most Gracious Majesty, of the one part, and to the said Indians of the other. . . ."[7] The Lieutenant-Governor and the Commissioner assured the Anishinabe that the Queen wished for what was best for them and found that the Anishinabe believed in this sentiment: "Indians in both parts have a firm belief in the honour and integrity of Her Majesty's representatives, and are fully impressed with the idea that the amelioration of their present condition is one of the objects of Her Majesty in making these treaties."[8]

Given the significance of kinship relationships among the Anishinabe, and given the extensive reliance by both parties on the mother/child relationship in the negotiations, we must inquire into the expectations implied by that relationship. What were the responsibilities of the mother toward her children, and what were the parameters of that relationship? What were the expectations of the Anishinabe in relation to the Queen?[9]

Obligations of love, kindness, and caring were invoked. These obligations entail duties to treat children equally, to listen to their needs and wants, and to provide for them in a loving and kind way. Given that the Anishinabe viewed their relationship with the Queen as one of kinship, they may have expected that the Queen would ensure equality among her "children" (the Anishinabe and the settlers). They may have also expected that their needs, if expressed to the Queen, would be met and that she would endeavour to create a good life for her children, while respecting their autonomy.

Obligations of Love, Kindness, and Understanding

The outline for a mother's obligations is found, for example, in the relationship between *Nimaamaa Aki* (Mother Earth) and the Anishinabe: to love and care for her children, to ensure that each of them are cared for: [10]

What it takes is the time and effort of any human being to be able to sit down on Mother Earth and learn to read the laws that we are to abide by if we are to have a happy life. All the laws of Mother Earth are based on respect, love, kindness and sharing. They are all positive — they teach us that we are all connected.[11]

The role of the mother, in accordance with Anishinabe laws, is to love her child unconditionally and to be kind and caring.[12] The Anishinabe *in-aakonigewin* of kindness is explained in the following way by Elder Ken Courchene:

> *ji-minode'ed Anishinaabe* [the people should have good hearts]. Truly your heart, your kindness. And he talked about that. The work that he does, not so much for himself but he wants to do his very best to ensure that there is a future for his child and grandchild. And he has that in his heart. And that's the third law, that kindness.[13]

Kindness is equated with care for others, in particular children and grandchildren. It is something that is carried in a person's heart. As Chief Ayeeta-pe-pe-tung had explained, "I hold my own very sacred, and therefore, could not work while my child is sitting in the dark."[14]

The mother is responsible for her child's immediate well-being, but is also responsible to ensure that her children are able to lead a good life into adulthood. The role of the mother is to nurture her child only to the extent that she will not impede her child's ability to be autonomous. The level of autonomy is measured by the level of ability of the child in each particular circumstance. It is reasonable to infer that the Anishinabe would have understood this in the context of the treaty as a requirement for the Queen to provide for the Anishinabe and to assist them while respecting their autonomy. In return, the child must listen to, care for, and respect his or her mother. This relationship is learned by observing the way *Nimaamaa Aki* treats her Anishinabe children — with love, kindness, and caring:

> Food was for everyone, humans, birds, animals, insects and fish, for this generation, the next and all those that followed. Mother Earth gave and gave. No matter how much she gave, Mother Earth's breadbasket never gave out.[15]

Even in fostering autonomy, the mother's responsibilities to her child always remain, they never end.[16] The sacred teaching of *Abenonjji Kakikwe Win* (roughly translated as "the teachings that are given to a child, that will last forever and that can only be given by a woman") prescribes that the teachings that a mother gives to her child enable the child to lead *mino-bimaadiziwin* (a good life). These teachings recognize the values of autonomy[17] and the child's individual quest for his or her vision, independently from the collective or the family unit, while always considering those collectivities in the exercise of autonomy and agency:

> To reproduce the qualities prized in a traditional leader — respect, honesty, truth, wisdom, bravery, love, and humility — our ancestors practiced relationships with children that embodied kindness, gentleness, patience, and love. Children were respected as people, they were encouraged to follow their visions and to realize their full potential while living up to the responsibilities of their families, communities, and nations. This was the key to creating leaders with integrity, creating good governance, and teaching future leaders how to interact in a respectful manner with other human and nonhuman nations.[18]

J. R. Miller argues that the importance of preserving a child's autonomy was not understood by the Crown representatives. Protection and assistance were mistaken for dependence and submission. For the Anishinabe, "language of family relations, including childhood, stemmed from a society in which youth was a time of autonomy during which children could count on protection and assistance from adult family members. It was not, as it was in Euro-Canadian society, a time of dependence and submission, a time to be 'seen but not heard.'"[19] Under British law, children were generally not considered to have rights. Although this was changing in the late 19th century, with legislation relating to mandatory school attendance and labour standards for young factory workers, for centuries children in British law had been property under the control of their parents until marriage or the age of majority.

During the negotiations, Wa-sus-koo-koon reminded the negotiators of the benevolence and good wishes of their "Great Mother," which would require that they be fed well during the negotiations and beyond.[20] The duty of care to children was not limited to the next generation, nor to the following one, but to the descendants to come, for an extended period of time, often referred to by the Anishinabe conceptually as thinking seven generations into the future. It also allowed for the autonomy of the Anishinabe, as was reflected in other procedural norms relied on in the Treaty One negotiations.

The relationship between mother and child may help to uncover some of the assumptions that were at play during the Treaty One negotiations. Although we cannot conclusively say that the Queen was regarded by the Anishinabe as a mother in more than metaphorical terms, the extensive reliance on the kinship terms by both parties likely had an impact on the understandings that were derived from the negotiations.

Dibishkoo (Equality) Among the Children

Once the relationship of kinship was established, the Queen's representatives assured the Anishinabe that, as the children of the Queen, they would not be treated differently from their mother's other children, including her White children.

> The old settlers and the settlers coming in, must be dealt with on the principles of fairness and justice as well as yourselves. Your Great Mother knows no difference between any of her people.[21]

> Your Great Mother wishes the good of all races under her sway. She wishes her Red Children, as well as her White people, to be happy and contented. She wishes them to live in comfort.[22]

The relationship was described as being founded on "that kindness of heart which distinguished her dealings with her red children. . . ."[23] This equal treatment of children was not limited to concepts of equality between the Queen's Red and White children, but extended also to equality in treatment of all her Indigenous "children."

The principle of equality between all persons is fundamental to Anishinabe *inaakonigewin*. For the Anishinabe, equality is expressed "through sharing, borrowing, and mutual exchange."[24]

> The seventh law, *nashke imaa gaa-gii-waakaabiyang* [look at how we sat in a circle]. *Bebakaan* [All differently]. We got to sit in this way. Everyone is different and yet equal. And we always had that belief, that difference is not to segregate someone is [sic] higher or lower.[25]

The Anishinabe considered the Queen's equal treatment of her children "from east to west" as an expression of the relationship of sustenance and reliance that was developed in their treaty alliance. If the Queen was to be a mother, all of her children would be treated equally, both by her and among themselves. Chief Ka-kee-ga-by-ness illustrated the principles of reciprocity, mutual obligation, and equality which applied to their relationship with the Queen as mother and also with regard to her other children:

> I salute my Great Mother, and am very much gratified at what I heard yesterday. I take all my Great Mother's children here by the hand and welcome them. I am very much pleased that myself and children are to be clothed by the Queen, and on that account welcome every white man into the country.[26]

It appears that the concept of equality between all people, as perceived in accordance with Anishinabe values, may have been imperfectly understood by the Crown negotiators. British law in the 19th century created and allowed for differential treatment of children, based on birth order, gender, whether they were born of a marriage, their age, and other factors. Although Archibald had stated that the Queen would treat all of her children equally,[27] he wrote to the Secretary of State that annuities paid to the Indians might have to increase in consequence of the "magnificent territory we are appropriating here," as distinguished from the treaties made with the Anishinabe further east.[28]

Conclusion

As the foundational pillar of Anishinabe *inaakonigewin*, relationships are strong indicators of normative expectations and obligations that exist between parties. Anishinabe relationships are based in equality and profound respect for all parts of creation. This chapter has illustrated relationships that existed within the context of the Treaty One negotiations and how the normative understandings of the Anishinabe were reflected in their ways of speaking, acting, and interacting among themselves and with the Queen's representatives.

Since the making of treaty, the Anishinabe have described the treaty as a relationship with the Queen that allowed for a peaceful and mutually beneficial sharing of the land between the Anishinabe and White settlers. Anishinabe Elders recount how the Anishinabe pledged to the Creator to share the land with the Queen's other children, in accordance with principles of kinship, equality, and reciprocity.

Based on the kinship obligations that can be seen to exist in the relationship with the Queen as mother, she would be expected to treat the Anishinabe with kindness, listen to their needs and requests, and to help them lead *mino-bimaadiziwin*. The expectation that she would allow Chief Sheeship his plea, "grant me wherewith to make my living," and her express wish to have her Red children "happy and contented . . . to live in comfort" met the normative expectations of the relationship from an Anishinabe perspective.

The use of kinship words and concepts by both parties was infused with legal meaning and significance. If Anishinabe *inaakonigewin* is "all about relationships,"[29] the relationship between a mother and her children is an illustration of the legal principles that governed the negotiation of Treaty One. The reference to kinship relationships invoked obligations of love, kindness, and caring that rely on foundations of equality and reciprocity. The conclusions that might flow from this better understanding of the Anishinabe perspective include expectations that the Anishinabe would share in the Queen's "bounty and benevolence" equally with the Queen's White children, and that the kinship relationship — and its obligations — would extend to future generations of Anishinabe.

The mother and child relationship may or may not have been understood in the same way by each of the parties.[30] Nonetheless, the treaty commissioners used the kinship language to establish the terms of the treaty, understanding that these relationships would allow them to enter into treaty with the Anishinabe. Therefore, the Anishinabe kinship laws formed a pillar of the treaty alliance. This relationship to the Queen continues to be invoked post-treaty. It was invoked by Morris in his efforts to implement Treaty One when he became lieutenant-governor of Manitoba and the North-West Territories. Many Elders continue to assert that Treaty One was not made with Canada but directly with the Queen of England.

CHAPTER SIX

"The Land Cannot Speak for Itself":
Relationships To and About Land

Although some Anishinabe negotiators, such as Henry Prince, demonstrated knowledge about concepts of the sale and acquisition of land, others defined their relationship to the land very differently. Chief Ayee-ta-pe-pe-tung, "a tall old brave, who was naked all but the breech-clout, and had his body smeared with white earth . . . spoke well, and in a very talkative and vehement manner, constantly flourishing an eagle's wing which he holds."[1] The chief spoke to the Queen's negotiators about his "ownership" and his view that rather than owning it, he was *made of the land*.[2]

Other chiefs relayed their view that they had a sacred responsibility toward the land and that the future of the land was intimately linked to the future of Anishinabe children. "The land cannot speak for itself. We have to speak for it; and want to know fully how you are going to treat our children."[3] Chief Ayee-ta-pe-pe-tung explained that his land was a gift from creation and that he could not give an answer, as the future of his grandchildren was dark, based on the proposal before him:

> I am not going to say much. It is proposed that we should give answer. Today I must give it. You (addressing His Excellency) know me. When you first found this country, you saw me on my property. . . . I belong to the Little Camp Fire at the Portage. When you first saw me, you did not see anything with me. You saw no canopy over my head — only the house which Creation had given me. This day is like a darkness to me; I am not prepared to answer. All is darkness to me how to plan for the future welfare of my grandchildren.[4]

Lieutenant-Governor Archibald responded that "[t]here is a dark cloud before us too, because we do not know what you want. There is the same dark cloud before you, because you do not know what we want. What we desire is to rend these clouds asunder."[5]

For the Anishinabe, the relationship to the land, namely the adherence to views of belonging to the land, being made of the land, and being in a relationship with the land are key factors that informed the Anishinabe perspective and understanding of the negotiations.

Anishinabe Relationships with Land

The Anishinabe dependence on the land and reverence for *Nimaamaa Aki* (Mother Earth) affected how they understood their responsibilities to the land and their ability to enter into negotiations about it with outsiders. The Anishinabe were bound by obligations of care toward the land, thanksgiving to the land for its bounty, and understanding that the Creator had assigned individuals to the land. They were created of the land and belonged to it. There is a direct relationship with *Nimaamaa Aki*: "[t]he second law is that, the earth itself, mother earth, the grandmother."[6] She is seen as kin to the Anishinabe. The earth is described as a living being, a mother.

> They talked to Earth Mother as they would another person, as if the earth could hear and understand and talk back. They told her that she was beautiful, and thanked her for her bounty. Each spring they asked her to be as bounteous as in the past, and beseeched the Thunderbirds to keep Earth Mother fresh and fertile. That every being was indebted to Earth Mother was in their minds.[7]

Although other elements, spirits, and animals are referred to in kinship terms, there is only one mother — *Nimaamaa Aki*. When harvesting from the bounty of the earth, *asemaa* (tobacco) is offered to *Nimaamaa Aki* in thanksgiving. Seasonal prayers of thanksgiving are directed to *Nimaamaa Aki*, as are daily prayers:

> When we hunger, Mother Earth nourishes us. Whatever we need is there in abundance, more than enough to fill the wants and needs of every insect, bird, animal, fish, man and woman with fruit, vegetables, seeds and nectars.
>
> When we need to clothe our bodies from the sun, wind, rain, snow and insects, Mother Earth provides the means to cover our bodies.

95

She gives fat and pelt to the deer, beaver, moose, buffalo, rabbit and bear. They, our older brothers and sisters, lend us their coats. To care for ourselves, our families and our communities, Mother Earth yields the means by which we make our weapons, canoes, snowshoes, clothing, utensils, adornments and our homes.

When we need shelter from the winds, snows, storms, rains, cold and heat, there are woods, forests, valleys, mountains, bays, and inlets where insects, birds, animals and humans may find harbour, build their nests and dens, or erect their dwellings and found their villages and towns.

When we are sick and need care to nurse us back to health, Mother Earth's meadows, forests, and shorelines are lush with berries, plants, roots, seeds and resins that bear the elixir of health and life. Our ancestors called medicine "Mashki-aki," the strength of the earth for its capacity to infuse the enfeebled sick with energy and vitality.

When our spirits flag and are burdened with cares, worries, losses and sorrows, Mother Earth comforts us. She whispers and chants to the downhearted and dispirited through the tree tops, over the meadows, in cascades and rapids. It is a mother's soothing voice offering solace to the low in spirit. She whispers, "I love you. I care."[8]

There was an obligation to share in the bounty of the land with those in need, but there was also a corresponding obligation to acknowledge the primary attachment of those who had been placed on the land. The Anishinabe do not own the land. "We belong to the land." Others say, "we are made of the land."[9] Elder Francis Nepinak and Elder Mark Thompson speak about how the Anishinabe are made directly from *Nimaamaa Aki*.

Iwe daabishkoo gichi-gamiin, zaaga'iganiin, ziibiwan daabishkoo gimiskwiiyaab giwiiyawing bezhigon. Bezhigon nibi eteg omaa akiing, daabishkoo miskwi owe dinong. Dago owe gitigan baabishkoo wiinizisan.

The oceans, the lakes, the rivers, it's similar to a blood vein in your body. It's like that. It's like the water on earth is its blood. And the plants like hair. Also, the ground is the same as your flesh.[10]

Amii aanish imaa gaa-bagidinind Anishinaabe gaa-ozhichigaadeg owe
aki . . . gii-ikidowag e-gii-ozhiyaad amii ono Anishinaaben, azhahki
egii aabajidood. Amii wenji miskozid awe Anishinaabe gii-ikidowag,
wedi miinawaa gii-ozhichigaazo bezhig.

This is where the Anishinaabe was placed earth was built/created
[sic]. . . . The Creator was very mystical. It was said that the Creator
made the Anishinaabe. He used the dirt. That is why the Anishinaabe
is red, they said.[11]

Prior to the treaty (and for some time after), the Anishinabe were dispersed over the land and used a seasonal rounds model (or biseasonal
movement)[12] on the land — hunting and trapping in the winter in more
remote areas and gathering in the spring and summer for fishing and berry
picking, sugaring, etc.[13] At one time, most Anishinabe learned everything
they needed to know from the land:

Through the high places and low, Kitchi-Manitou shows us, speaks to
us. Our ancestors watched and listened. The land was their book. The
land has given us our understandings, beliefs, perceptions, laws, customs. It has bent and shaped our notions of human nature, conduct
and the Great Laws. And our ancestors tried to abide by those laws.
The land has given us everything.[14]

The areas used by certain groups for particular purposes were recognized
and respected by others, often subject to an annual allocation based on resource conditions. People were to take only what they needed. "This earth
is bountiful and rich. *Gii-manaajichigewag aaniish* [The people used to be
respectful]. The people were respectful. They only took what they needed,
everything in moderation. That's the way the spirits of the people were."[15]

The land was Mother Earth and her resources were her bounty. Where
land was not productive for harvesting, it would not be used. Simple ownership without use was meaningless. As Hallowell notes, there is no desire
amongst the Anishinabe to own or sell land:

[T]here is nothing in Saulteaux culture that motivates the possession
of land for land's sake. Usufruct, rather than the land itself, is an economic value and land is never rented or sold. The use of the land and

its products are a source of wealth rather than land ownership itself. There is no prestige whatsoever that accrues to the man who hunts over a large area. Nor is there any direct correlation between the size of the winter hunting group and the area of the hunting ground they occupy.[16]

Basil Johnston explains the attachment to a particular piece of land or territory in terms of a form of tenancy that is assigned by the Creator, rather than ownership or possession of land.[17] He also refers to *aeindauyaun* — "a place that belongs to me and where I long to be."[18] Treaty Commissioner Morris remarked that the "Indians have a strong attachment to the localities, in which they and their fathers have been accustomed to dwell, and it is desirable to cultivate this home feeling of attachment to the soil."[19]

Respect for another's use of land ensured that everyone would be cared for. "Within the territory set aside for nations, individuals and families occupied land that they regarded as their home 'ai-indauyaun', and which their neighbours granted as belonging to them, 'ae-indauwaut.'"[20]

> The Indian concept of land ownership is certainly not inconsistent with the idea of sharing with an alien people. Once the Indians recognized them as human beings, they gladly shared with them. They shared with Europeans in the same way they shared with the animals and other people. However, sharing here cannot be interpreted as meaning the Europeans got the same rights as any other native person, because the Europeans were not descendants of the original grantees, or they were not parties to the original social contract. Also, sharing certainly cannot be interpreted as meaning that one is giving up his rights for all eternity.[21]

The relationship to the land cannot be understood in isolation from the Anishinabe practices of treaty making and relationship building. This mutuality of caring and respect for each other's well-being, through the bounty of the land, is reflective of the relationship the Anishinabe have with the land. The land was meant to be shared among living beings:

> Dependence upon hunting, trapping and fishing for a living is precarious at best and, even though the individual hunter may exercise his best skills, it is impossible to accumulate food for the inevitable

rainy day. As a result, if I have more than I need today, I share it with you because I know that you, in turn, will share what you have with me tomorrow. In Ojibwa society there are no culturally structured incentives that induce individuals to surpass their fellow in the accumulation of material goods. No one is expected to have much more than anyone else, except temporarily.[22]

If people travel through Anishinabe territory, they are entitled to feed themselves.[23] This is the way of the Anishinabe. However, the outsider cannot take more than he needs. He must also share his catch with the Anishinabe. As *nimishomis* (my grandfather) put it, if he took three fish, he would share them by giving me two and keeping one for himself. "I know that I will catch more fish but I do not know that you will not go hungry."[24]

The language used by each of the parties in the treaty negotiations can provide some insight into the intentions and understandings of the parties.[25] The words of the Chiefs at the Treaty One negotiations echoed those of the late Chief Peguis:

> [T]hese are not my Lands — they belong to our Great Father for it is he only that gives us the means of existence, for what would become of us if he left us to ourselves — we would wither like the Grass in Plains was the Sun to withdraw his animating beams. . . .[26]

Conclusion

The Anishinabe did not surrender their land in the Treaty One negotiations. It was not in their power to do so, as they did not own it. In their eyes, they were in a sacred relationship with the land, endorsed by the Creator. In essence, the Crown viewed the treaty as a transfer of land — land that was under the control of the Anishinabe and which was greatly desired by settlers and the Crown. I use the word "control" here as a compromise between the concepts of ownership and jurisdiction from a western perspective, and the view of belonging to the land and being allowed to use the land from the Anishinabe perspective. The conceptual differences between these views of land were explained at the treaty negotiations, but it is unclear if either party truly understood the other's concepts of land and authority over its use. In fact, on the last day of the negotiations, Chief Ayee-ta-pe-pe-tung was prepared to have the land taken from him, rather than enter into a treaty he was not comfortable signing:

> I have turned over this matter of a treaty in my mind and cannot see anything in it to benefit my children. This is what frightens me. After I showed you what I meant to keep for a reserve, you continued to make it smaller and smaller. Now, I will go home today, to my own property, without being treated with. You (the Commissioner) can please yourself. I know our Great Mother the Queen is strong, and that we cannot keep back her power more than we can keep back the sun. If therefore the Commissioner wants the land, let him take it. . . . Let the Queen's subjects go on my land if they choose. I give them liberty. Let them rob me. I will go home without treating.[27]

PART 4

LIVING THE TREATY

CHAPTER SEVEN

Implementing the Treaty:
Outside Promises and Post-Treaty Disputes
in the Immediate Post-Treaty Years

Prior to the treaty negotiations, Simon Dawson had advised Ottawa about the Anishinabe and their ability to recall details of agreements, and their determinedness to observe their commitments:

> At these gatherings it is necessary to observe extreme caution in what is said, as, though they have no means of writing, there are always those present who are charged to keep every word in mind. As an instance of the manner in which the records are in this way kept, without writing, I may mention that, on one occasion, at Fort Frances, the principal Chief of the tribe commenced an oration, by repeating, almost verbatim, what I had said to him two years previously. . . .
>
> For my own part, I would have the fullest reliance as to these Indians observing a treaty and adhering most strictly to all its provisions, if, in the first place it were concluded after full discussion and after all its provisions were thoroughly understood by the Indians, and if, in the next, it were never infringed upon by the whites, who are generally the first to break through Indian treaties.[1]

We have seen that, based on the record of the negotiations, a great deal of time and effort was expended in the negotiations on the question of land ownership and the concept of "use of land." The continued use of the land by the Anishinabe for hunting and other harvesting purposes was not disputed. Confusion arose primarily over the concept of reserves. The record does not mention discussions about concepts such as cession, release, or surrender, terms that were later used in the treaty text to effect the purported surrender of land. The evidence shows that up until the last day of the negotiations, the Anishinabe were prepared to walk away from them. While it is unclear what was said, or what promises or assurances were delivered to entice them into signing the treaty on August 3, 1871, the fact remains that the Anishinabe were never recorded to have agreed to a complete surrender of land. The Anishinabe reserved the right to continue to use the land, to manage it and to share it with the White settlers. In relation to reserves, they were to be lands reserved exclusively for the purposes of agriculture, for when the Anishinabe chose to take up farming.

Almost immediately after the making of Treaty One, correspondence from Anishinabe leaders highlighted their understanding of the terms of the treaty. Many of the chiefs wrote or met with government officials to express their dissatisfaction with outside attempts to regulate their natural resource use. In addition, outside promises, which had been recorded in a memorandum attached to the commissioner's treaty report, were not implemented. Protestations and complaints were made by the chiefs, including their refusal to take annuity payments or to select reserves. Lieutenant-Governor Morris was forced to re-negotiate the outside promises into the treaty in 1875.

Very few opportunities were given to reconcile the divergent understandings of the treaty. Sarah Carter finds that treaties were "confirmed and ratified in the years that followed through audiences and ceremonies held with the Queen's representatives."[2] Carter argues that the audience and ceremonies were used by the Indigenous parties to "restate and recommit the equal parties to the treaties, and to remind their treaty partner of their commitments and obligations"[3] and of "grievances to be addressed."[4] Yet it appears today that the parties to the treaty still understand their commitments in very different ways, their respective grievances having yet to be addressed.

Outside Promises and Post-Treaty Disputes

Almost immediately following the making of the treaty, the Anishinabe complained about the non-implementation of the treaty promises, and identified promises that had not been included in the written text of the treaty. "This, naturally, led to misunderstanding with the Indians, and to widespread dissatisfaction among them."[5] The Indians constantly corresponded and met with the Lieutenant-Governor, and when the Minister of the Interior, David Laird, came to Manitoba, they "pressed their demands on him."[6] When Lieutenant-Governor Morris attended the locations of the bands to pay them, in some cases, the money was not accepted.[7] Others prepared to visit Ottawa and some petitioned the Governor General, the Earl of Dufferin. In 1874, the Portage band sent messengers with *asemaa* twice to Qu'Appelle to tell Indians in that area not to make a treaty with the Crown.[8]

A list of the outside promises had been appended as a memorandum[9] to the treaty but had not made its way into Simpson's official report of the negotiations. They were, therefore, never ratified by the Privy Council. In 1873, the government of Canada refused to acknowledge the complaints or to address them substantively: "Unless it could be shown that this treaty was unjust or unfair, or was obtained by unfair means, it must be maintained."[10] Later, in the face of uncertainty about their ability to negotiate further treaties, and at Morris's insistence, the Privy Council agreed to consider the memorandum as part of the treaty and raised the annuity to $5, in exchange for the abandonment of all claims relating to verbal promises other than those contained in the memorandum. In 1875, Treaty Commissioner Alexander Morris proceeded to re-negotiate the treaty with the bands to include the items listed in the memorandum. These included: dress and buggies for the chiefs and two of their braves and councillors (except for Chief Yellow Quill), a bull and a boar for each reserve, a cow and a sow for each chief, and ploughs and harrows for "each settler cultivating the ground." In exchange, "any Indian accepting the increased payment, thereby formally abandoned all claims against the Government, in connection with the verbal promises of the Commissioners, other than those recognized by the treaty and the memorandum referred to."[11] Chief Yellow Quill referred to these negotiations as "the second treaty." There is no record of the 1875 negotiations or the discussions surrounding the abandonment of all claims against the Government.

In 1875, the outside promises were acknowledged and included in the treaty because they formed part of the official record. They are another written form of treaty. It also appears from the oral history and the written records that additional promises were made, and that much of what was discussed appeared neither in the text of the treaty nor in the memorandum of outside promises: "You will observe in this that there are several matters not spoken of in the Treaty, or mentioned in the outside promises. . . ."[12]

It had been palpable from the first that the present unsatisfactory state of the relationship was inevitable, and Mr. Commissioner Simpson though always seeking to hide over any difficulty in the hopes that time would exercise its usual influence in such cases; has always expressed his regret at having allowed signing of the first Treaty to be rushed as it was, when as subsequent events have shown it was so necessary to have a perfect understanding. The full demands of the Indians cannot of course be complied with but there is nevertheless a certain paradox in asking a wild Indian who has hitherto gained his livelihood by hunting and trapping to settle down on a Reservation and cultivate the land without at the same time offering him some means of making his living. As they say themselves 'We cannot tear down trees and build huts with our teeth; we cannot break the Prairie with our hands nor reap the harvest when we have grown it with our knives.'[13]

Post-treaty assertions made by the chiefs from various Treaty One bands confirmed the view that natural resources, such as game and fish, had not been given up in the treaty. According to Chief Asham, it was "understood thoroughly and distinctly in regard about game that no Indian was to be prohibited killing or catching for is [sic] own purpose any kind of game all year round."[14] A similar sentiment was echoed by the chief and councillors at Fort Alexander who wrote to Canada that the "Indians under Treaty were permitted to enjoy all privileges of hunting and fishing for their own use and benefit in perpetuity without payment of any licence or fee for game, fish, nets, or hunting implements."[15] Similarly, Chief Naskepenais protested the application of regulations that infringed their treaty right or prevented them from taking fish. He expressed that they had "no intention of rebelling against or defying the laws of the land but merely to state that as fishing regulations are against the conditions of 'treaty' we cannot accept of them and shall therefore not consider ourselves bound to observe these laws by abstaining from taking fish for their own use."[16] The chiefs and councillors of Brokenhead expressed their view that fish had been reserved from them in Treaty One and that they could sell "their" fish without payment or penalty. Chief Naskepenais and his Councillors explained that they "did not sell our fish, this commodity we reserved for our own exclusive benefit. The fish then being clearly our own we cannot but come to the conclusion that we can sell it to whomsoever we choose without paying license."[17]

When Chief Yellow Quill was warned in 1885 not to kill deer, he "neither admitted nor denied the charge but merely laughed and said if he was starving and saw a Deer he would certainly shoot it and that if the Government wanted to prevent them killing Game they must feed them as they had nothing to live on. . . . unless they were allowed to kill Game they would starve."[18]

The confusion about the concept of reserves continued after the treaty, in particular in relation to reserve selections. In 1876 when Morris, Indian Commissioner Provencher, and McKay visited the Portage band and asked them to select reserves, "they did not understand its extent, and claimed nearly half of the Province of Manitoba under it."[19] Yellow Quill said that "he did not understand the extent of the reserve."[20]

Three years after the treaty negotiations, Chief Wa-quse[21] wrote to Lieutenant-Governor Morris: "[T]hey don't follow the agreement at all, it is not for three dollars a head that I would have sold my land. I dindt [sic] sold neither signed the treaty before they had promised me what I asked but now they don't even give us enough to eat."[22]

The frequency and detailed nature of post-treaty complaints by the Treaty One chiefs can lead to the assumption that, in addition to the outside promises added to the treaty in 1875, there were other promises that may not have been recorded in Commissioner Simpson's report.[23] The negotiated agreement was likely far more nuanced than the reported terms of a treaty rooted in surrender of land in exchange for annuities and goods.

Re-kindling the Fire:

Finding and Embracing the Spirit and Intent

of Treaty One Today

There are things that were not on the table at Treaty: Sovereignty, Treaty making power and membership . . . conditional access in exchange for health, education, shelter — the three main things that we entered into Treaty One for.[1]

A better understanding can be achieved not only through the interpretive lenses provided by archives and western readings of those archives, but by considering the Anishinabe perspective on the treaty negotiations. Informed by contextual factors, this perspective includes a body of substantive and procedural legal principles that helped make the treaty. Treaties are agreements to enter into relationship. Although it is tempting to examine treaties with a view to identifying shared understandings or common ground, this cannot give us a full understanding of treaty. The idea that interaction between European and Indigenous parties resulted in a "middle ground"[2] or "intersocietal law"[3] have limited application in the context of the Treaty One negotiations. Indigenous and non-Indigenous legal traditions did not blend and form a new, distinctive, or hybrid form of law on which the parties would have relied. Rather, there were two systems of law in operation, the Anishinabe having their own system of law and the Crown another. By adopting both procedural and substantive forms of Anishinabe *inaakonigewin* (law) in the context of the negotiations, the Crown representatives engaged the legal framework which was rich with normative meaning for the Anishinabe. Although the Crown representatives may not have understood that they were adopting and operating in an Anishinabe legal tradition, this does not change the fact that the Anishinabe had a particular understanding of the treaty negotiations, informed by their system of law, that continues to guide Anishinabe interpretation of treaty today. While European and Indigenous people on Turtle Island may have developed a middle ground of cultural interaction, on the legal front, the creation of a common form of law between the Crown and the Anishinabe likely took place post-treaty without having been fully defined or solidified in advance of or at the Treaty One negotiations.

This being the case, it is not acceptable to consider the subsequent interpretation and implementation of the treaty only in terms of Canadian common law. The Anishinabe laws underlying the negotiations and the subsequent formation of the treaty agreement must be recognized and considered in the interpretation and implementation of the treaty.

The written text of the treaty, the historical record, and the verbal statements made at the treaty negotiations indicate that the Crown wished to settle western Canada with the consent of the Indigenous inhabitants. The policy was to make treaties with the Indigenous people on behalf of the Queen, and to ensure peace and good will between Indigenous people and the Crown, in exchange for the Queen's "bounty and benevolence."[4] As the Supreme Court of Canada stated in relation to historic treaties, "the treaty was concluded orally and subsequently reduced to writing. The oral promises made when the treaty was agreed to are as much a part of the treaty as the written words."[5] Each of the parties to the treaty brought into the negotiation circle objectives, viewpoints, and systems of law and governance which, in many instances, were vastly different from those of the other party.

I have argued that the true spirit and intent of the treaty can be explored and perhaps ultimately resolved by understanding the systems of law that informed the treaty negotiations. In turn, such understandings can foster better interpretations of the treaty that will allow for more fruitful attempts at treaty implementation. Unfortunately, the practice of privileging Western law over Anishinabe *inaakonigewin* has negatively affected current approaches to treaty interpretation. In particular, Treaty One remains to be fully understood from the Anishinabe perspective. Like any other system of law, Anishinabe *inaakonigewin* changes over time, responding to the particular context and circumstances of the Anishinabe. Adopting fixed and rigid understandings of law would not allow us to give effect to the treaty in a way that recognizes that it is an evolving relationship which rests on the commitment to renewal and the possibility of evolving implementation based in a respectful and reciprocal implementation of treaty.

In trying to understand Treaty One, some questions remain difficult to answer, given the current and historical divergence of the parties' perspectives:

- What was intended to be the effect of Treaty One on the lands? Was it surrender, sale, shared use of land? What was to be retained by the Anishinabe?
- How was the concept of reserves explained and understood?
- What was the nature of the treaty relationship?

As illustrated in Chapter 1, the Anishinabe had interacted with the fur traders for over a century and a half, in relationships of kinship and trade that were grounded in Anishinabe values and customs. For example, by smoking the pipe together, the parties to a trade treaty made a substantive commitment to speak truthfully and maintain good relations. At the Treaty One negotiations, Commissioner Simpson relied on the existing relationship with the Hudson's Bay Company and the physical location of the HBC fort to ensure fruitful negotiations.[6] In addition to building on the existing relationships with the HBC, the prior practices of treaty negotiation between the Crown and the Anishinabe informed the making of Treaty One. Each of the treaties between the Anishinabe and the Crown set the table for the negotiations, building upon the principles established in the *Royal Proclamation of 1763*. For example, the Treaty of Niagara was conducted, at least in part, in accordance with Anishinabe protocols and laws. This continued in later treaty making. In particular, the non-interference and mutual assistance that are illustrated by the Covenant Chain Belt and the Two Row Wampum Belts help to further illustrate the perspective that the Anishinabe brought to their negotiation of Treaty One.

At the outset of the Treaty One negotiations, assurances were made by the Crown that land and resource use by the Anishinabe would continue, and that the use of land for settlers would be limited to agriculture. At no point in the negotiations is it recorded, in any document or in the oral histories, that the parties discussed the concepts of land surrender or sale. The assurances of continued land use without interference constitute a recognition of Anishinabe jurisdiction over and primary right of use of the resources and the land. The terms of the settlers' agricultural use were guaranteed not to interfere in any fundamental way with the Anishinabe way of life. As stated by Lieutenant-Governor Archibald in his opening remarks, "There will still be plenty of land that is neither tilled nor occupied where you can go and roam and hunt as you have always done."[7] Elder Victor Courchene explains that the Anishinabe and the settlers would eat on a plate together:

> One old man, much older than me, said his grandfather told him about the Treaty and how it was supposed to work. He said it is like a plate and the resources were on that plate. The white man was invited to come and eat from that plate together with the Anishinabe. This is how he understood the Treaty. They never gave up anything.[8]

These words are very instructive about the way the Anishinabe understood and intended the sharing of the land and resources. Eating from a plate together does not mean dividing the food, re-distributing it or eating separately from one another — it means to eat at the same time. This, blended with concepts such as ensuring that the other or the visitor will be fed, and caring for others, allows us to better understand how the idea of sharing was not equated to cession, release, or surrender. Let us be clear that sharing did not mean giving up land and resources, but, rather, it meant using the land and resources together.

In many instances, the written record does not detail the discussions or explanations that took place, including the content of the chiefs' speeches and the "very full explanations in Indian"[9] by James McKay. It is possible that these explanations were not aimed at explaining to the Anishinabe the intentions of the Crown through the lens of Western concepts but were for the purpose of explaining the negotiations in terms that would be conceptually understood by the Anishinabe. When the Lieutenant-Governor spoke of "God's will" that the land be cultivated, the translation and understanding of those concepts through the eyes of the Anishinabe would have been very different, given the understandings of their relationship to land and the resources that were placed upon it by the Creator for their use.

While early on in the negotiations the chiefs claimed two-thirds of the treaty area as reserves, the concept of "reserves" was further explained to them (the content of these explanations is not on the record), and pressure was exercised by the negotiators. The Anishinabe are purported to have agreed to the creation of reserves for their use, although we can conceive from the record that these reserves were understood to be for their use as agricultural lands (if they chose to engage in agriculture), while not limiting their other existing resource use. Part of the divergent understandings about the purpose of reserves may be related to assumptions that the Anishinabe would eventually set aside hunting and trapping in favour of agriculture. While both the Anishinabe and Crown negotiators viewed the treaty as being related to land, the Anishinabe perspective differed and the treaty agreement was approached according to the view that relationship, rather than possession, dictated use of land. The Anishinabe view was rooted in an attachment to the land, based on use assigned by the Creator. There was also an underlying obligation to share in the bounty of the earth with other brothers and sisters, which helps explain the Anishinabe willingness to enter into a sharing treaty, not unlike models they had developed with the fur traders over the previous centuries.

The written text of the treaty contemplates that the Anishinabe obligation under the treaty would be "to maintain perpetual peace between themselves and Her Majesty's White subjects, and not to interfere with the property or in any way molest the persons of Her Majesty's white or other subjects."[10] From the Crown's perspective, although not detailed in the text of the treaty or in the negotiations, a total and complete surrender and acquisition of land was contemplated. The Anishinabe did not view Treaty One as a sale of land, but as an agreement to share in its bounty. At the negotiations, the Anishinabe expressed a clear attachment to the land and responsibility toward the land, as illustrated by the remarks of the chiefs. These views would have come into direct conflict with concepts of sale and surrender of land. Also, a total surrender of land would have been fundamentally incompatible with continued use of the land for hunting, trapping, fishing, and other types of harvesting, as such activities entail planning and resource management. The written record of the negotiations is consistent with the Anishinabe understanding of their legal relationship to the land. As illustrated in Ayee-ta-pe-pe-tung's translated speech to the Treaty Commissioners, he was made of the land:

> When first you began to travel from Fort William you saw something afar off and this is the land you saw. At that time you thought I will have that some day or other; but behold you see before you the lawful owner of it. I understand you are going to buy this land from me. Well

God made me out of this very clay that is besmeared on my body. This is what you say you are going to buy from me.[11]

In his analysis of Treaty Nine, John Long concludes that "aboriginal title and Indigenous rights were not knowingly ceded, released, surrendered, or yielded up by the Ojibwe and Cree. Indigenous peoples agreed to accept presents that to them signified a renewal of their commitment to the fur trade's middle ground of compromise and coexistence."[12]

Although much pressure and many threats were employed by the Crown in the negotiations, the chiefs repeatedly expressed hesitation to enter into the relationship, saying that some of the treaty terms were unclear to them. Where demands were made by the Anishinabe, in particular on the last day of the negotiations, there is no explicit reference on the record of those demands having been granted or refused. We cannot know what induced the Anishinabe to change their minds and conclude the treaty after they had announced their departure, other than to speculate that they were re-assured by McKay that their position would be protected. We do know that general dissatisfaction with the implementation of the treaty on the part of the Anishinabe began almost immediately after the signing.

It is reasonable to assume that Anishinabe understandings and norma-tive expectations would have infused the discussions at the negotiations, including the fundamental discussions about land tenure and use. The di-rect assurances of non-interference resonated with the Anishinabe norma-tive principles of non-interference, and likely engaged expectations about how that non-interference would take shape on the land. First, the Anishi-nabe expected they would not be limited in their movements or their sus-tenance activities, and second, they understood that they could take up ag-riculture and settle on lands set aside for them for that purpose, in the form of reserves. Both the Anishinabe understanding of land and resources, and their relationship to Mother Earth and the Creator supported continued Anishinabe jurisdiction over land and natural resources. Neither an owner nor a seller, the Anishinabe used the land and cared for it. The Anishinabe retained control over the land, subject to sharing it with the White settlers for the limited purpose of sustenance. In return for the sharing of land, the mother had obligations of love, kindness, and caring toward her children, which entailed listening to their wants and providing for their needs, in order for them to have *mino-bimaadiziwin* (a good life). The expressions of kinship with the Queen were likely invoked in part to ensure equality among the children (including the settlers), as well as an expectation that their needs, if expressed to the Queen, would be met and that she would endeavour to create a good life for her children. These obligations were to continue into the future and apply to future generations, as was illustrated by many of the chiefs' speeches.

In Anishinabe *inaakonigewin*, relationships never end. They are constantly fostered, re-defined, re-examined, and re-negotiated. They must be tended, fuelled, nurtured, or simmered. They morph and evolve over time. The treaty is a relationship which has no end. As Elder Elmer Courchene describes it, "the fire is lowered, until the next time we meet. We have not finished our work. Our work is never done. Things change, we change. We will discuss this again."[13]

> Traditionally, First Nations did not allocate property in the exercise of their treaty decision-making powers by conducting their relationship with other people in a static way. Relationships were continually renewed and reaffirmed through ceremonial customs. Renewal and re-interpretation were practised to bring past agreements into harmony with changing circumstances. First Nations preferred this articulation of treaty-making to exercise their powers of self-government because it was consistent with their oral tradition. The idea of the principles of a treaty being "frozen" through terms written on paper was an alien concept.[14]

To look at the treaties as one isolated moment in time, independent of the past or the future, is not in keeping with the Anishinabe perspective. The treaty was a relationship developed on the basis of respect and was intended to last "as long as the grass grows, the sun shines and the rivers flow."[15] Therefore, the lowering of the fire post-negotiation, and changes in circumstances over the years, should not imply the extinguishment of the treaty, but merely that the relationship needs tending. Treaties are presumed to have been negotiated in good faith. Their provisions were to be implemented faithfully.

How then are the two treaty perspectives to be reconciled? Treaties are agreements between two parties in which neither perspective should be privileged over the other. A better understanding of the Anishinabe perspective flows from considering Anishinabe laws, both procedural and substantive, that informed and impacted the treaty negotiations. These understandings may assist the current generation and descendants of the treaty parties in their quest for understanding how the interpretations are divergent and how they may one day be reconciled. Elmer Courchene explains: "Those resources are out there. Those resources are the resources that were taken away from us. The governments have to be able to sit down and begin to talk about sharing these resources with us."[16]

There is an Anishinabe prophecy which foretells significant environmental change. Today, Mother Earth is suffering and the sharing of the land has not taken place in accordance with the values that were set out at the treaty negotiations:

> Ji-naagadawaabamangitiwaa ongo gaa-bi-dagoshinowaad. Gi-gii-bakwenimaanaanik gi-dakiinaan owe ginookomisinaan. Nashke dash gaa-doodamowaad. Noongom da-gekise. Gaawiin gaye ginezh aazha aanish gii-dibaajimo ongo gaa-bawajigewaad, dibaajimo ako aadi-zookaanag.

> We shared our grandmother with them. But look at what they did to our grandmother. It will change today. It will not be long now, as it was shared by the ones who have visions that the spirit helpers are sharing [with us].[17]

The prophecy also speaks of hope for a change in the relationship. My hope is that a better understanding of Anishinabe normative values and principles will assist in rebuilding the treaty relationship and allow us to honour its original spirit and intent. The core purpose of treaty was to create relationships, not to cede land — which was the way that it was understood by the Anishinabe and endorsed by the Creator.

Treaty No. 1

ARTICLES OF A TREATY made and concluded this third day of August in the year of Our Lord one thousand eight hundred and seventy-one, between Her Most Gracious Majesty the Queen of Great Britain and Ireland by Her Commissioner, Wemyss M. Simpson, Esquire, of the one part, and the Chippewa and Swampy Cree Tribes of Indians, inhabitants of the country within the limits hereinafter defined and described, by their Chiefs chosen and named as hereinafter mentioned, of the other part.

Whereas all the Indians inhabiting the said country have pursuant to an appointment made by the said Commissioner, been convened at a meeting at the Stone Fort, otherwise called Lower Fort Garry, to deliberate upon certain matters of interest to Her Most Gracious Majesty, of the one part, and to the said Indians of the other, and whereas the said Indians have been notified and informed by Her Majesty's said Commissioner that it is the desire of Her Majesty to open up to settlement and immigration a tract of country bounded and described as hereinafter mentioned, and to obtain the consent thereto of her Indian subjects inhabiting the said tract, and to make a treaty and arrangements with them so that there may be peace and good will between them and Her Majesty, and that they may know and be assured of what allowance they are to count upon and receive year by year from Her Majesty's bounty and benevolence.

And whereas the Indians of the said tract, duly convened in council as aforesaid, and being requested by Her Majesty's said Commissioner to name certain Chiefs and headmen who should be authorized on their behalf to conduct such negotiations and sign any treaty to be founded thereon, and to become responsible to Her Majesty for the faithful performance by their respective bands of such obligations as should be assumed by them, the said Indians have thereupon named the following persons for that purpose, that is to say:

Mis-koo-ke-new or Red Eagle (Henry Prince), Ka-ke-ka-penais, or Bird for ever, Na-sha-kepenais, or Flying down bird, Na-na-wa-nanaw, or Centre of Bird's Tail, Ke-we-tayash, or Flying round, Wa-ko-wush, or Whippoor-will, Oo-za-we-kwun, or Yellow Quill,—and thereupon in open council the different bands have presented their respective Chiefs to His Excellency the Lieutenant Governor of the Province of Manitoba and of the North-West Territory being present at such council, and to the said Commissioner, as the Chiefs and Headman for the purposes aforesaid of the respective bands of Indians inhabiting the said district hereinafter described; and whereas the said Lieutenant Governor and the said Commissioner then and there received and acknowledged the persons so presented as Chiefs and Headmen for the purpose aforesaid; and whereas the said Commissioner has proceeded to negotiate a treaty with the said Indians, and the same has finally been agreed upon and concluded as follows, that is to say:

The Chippewa and Swampy Cree Tribes of Indians and all other the Indians inhabiting the district hereinafter described and defined do hereby cede, release, surrender and yield up to Her Majesty the Queen and successors forever all the lands included within the following limits, that is to say:

Beginning at the international boundary line near its junction with the Lake of the Woods, at a point due north from the centre of Roseau Lake; thence to run due north to the centre of Roseau Lake; thence northward to the centre of White Mouth Lake, otherwise called White Mud Lake; thence by the middle of the lake and the middle of the river issuing therefrom to the mouth thereof in Winnipeg River; thence by the Winnipeg River to its mouth; thence westwardly, including all the islands near the south end of the lake, across the lake to the mouth of Drunken River; thence westwardly to a point on Lake Manitoba half way between Oak Point and the mouth of Swan Creek; thence across Lake Manitoba in a line due west to its western shore; thence in a straight line to the crossing of the rapids on the Assiniboine; thence due south to the international boundary line; and thence eastwardly by the said line to the place of beginning. To have and to hold the same to Her said Majesty the Queen and Her successors for ever; and Her Majesty the Queen hereby agrees and undertakes to lay aside and reserve for the sole and exclusive use of the Indians the following tracts of land, that is to say: For the use of the Indians belonging to the band of which Henry Prince, otherwise called Mis-koo-ke-new is the Chief, so much of land on both sides of the Red River, beginning at the south line of St. Peter's Parish, as will furnish one hundred and sixty acres for each family of five, or in that proportion for larger or smaller families; and for the use of the Indians of whom Na-sha-ke-penais, Na-na-wa-nanaw, Ke-we-tayash and Wa-ko-wush are the Chiefs, so much land on the Roseau River as will furnish one hundred and sixty acres for each family of five, or in that proportion for larger or smaller families, beginning from the mouth of the river; and for the use of the Indians of which Ka-ke-ka-penais is the Chief, so much land on the Winnipeg River above Fort Alexander as will furnish one hundred and sixty acres for each family of five, or in that proportion for larger or smaller families, beginning at a distance of a mile or thereabout above the Fort; and for the use of the Indians of whom Oo-zawe-kwun is Chief, so much land on the south and east side of the Assiniboine, about twenty miles above the Portage, as will furnish one hundred and sixty acres for each family of five, or in that proportion for larger or smaller families, reserving also a further tract enclosing said reserve to comprise an equivalent to twenty-five square miles of equal breadth, to be laid out round the reserve, it being understood, however, that if, at the date of the execution of this treaty, there are any settlers within the bounds of any lands reserved by any band, Her Majesty reserves the right to deal with such settlers as She shall deem just, so as not to diminish the extent of land allotted to the Indians.

And with a view to show the satisfaction of Her Majesty with the behaviour and good conduct of Her Indians parties to this treaty, She hereby, through Her Commissioner, makes them a present of three dollars for each Indian man, woman and child belonging to the bands here represented.

And further, Her Majesty agrees to maintain a school on each reserve hereby made whenever the Indians of the reserve should desire it.

Within the boundary of Indian reserves, until otherwise enacted by the proper legislative authority, no intoxicating liquor shall be allowed to be introduced or sold, and all laws now in force or hereafter to be enacted to preserve Her Majesty's Indian subjects inhabiting the reserves or living elsewhere from the evil influence of the use of intoxicating liquors shall be strictly enforced.

Her Majesty's Commissioner shall, as soon as possible after the execution of this treaty, cause to be taken an accurate census of all the Indians inhabiting the district above described, distributing them in families, and shall in every year ensuing the date hereof, at some period during the month of July in each year, to be duly notified to the Indians and at or near their respective reserves, pay to each Indian family of five persons the sum of fifteen dollars Canadian currency, or in like proportion for a larger or smaller family, such payment to be made in such articles as the Indians shall require of blankets, clothing, prints (assorted colours), twine or traps, at the current cost price in Montreal, or otherwise, if Her Majesty shall deem the same desirable in the interests of Her Indian people, in cash.

And the undersigned Chiefs do hereby bind and pledge themselves and their people strictly to observe this treaty and to maintain perpetual peace between themselves and Her Majesty's white subjects, and not to interfere with the property or in any way molest the persons of Her Majesty's white or other subjects.

IN WITNESS WHEREOF, Her Majesty's said Commissioner and the said Indian Chiefs have hereunto subscribed and set their hand and seal at Lower Fort Garry, this day and year herein first above named.

Signed, sealed and delivered in the presence of, the same having been first read and explained:
ADAMS G. ARCHIBALD,
Lieut.-Gov. of Man. and
N.W. Territories.
JAMES McKAY, P.L.C.
A. G. IRVINE, Major
ABRAHAM COWLEY,
DONALD GUNN, M.L.C.
THOMAS HOWARD, P.S.
HENRY COCHRANE,
JAMES McARRISTER,
HUGH McARRISTER,
E. ALICE ARCHIBALD,
HENRI BOUTHILLIER.

WEMYSS M. SIMPSON, [L.S.]
Indian Commissioner,
MIS-KOO-KEE-NEW, or
RED EAGLE
(HENRY PRINCE),
    his x mark
KA-KE-KA-PENAIS (or BIRD FOR
EVER),
WILLIAM PENNEFATHER,
    his x mark
NA-SHA-KE-PENNAIS, or
FLYING DOWN BIRD,
    his x mark
NA-HA-WA-NANAN, or
CENTRE OF BIRD'S TAIL,
    his x mark

KE-WE-TAY-ASH,
or FLYINGROUND,
his x mark
WA-KO-WUSH,
or WHIP-POOR-WILL,
his x mark
OO-ZA-WE-KWUN,
or YELLOW QUILL,
his x mark

Memorandum of things outside of the Treaty which were promised at the Treaty at the Lower Fort, signed the third day of August, A.D. 1871.

• For each Chief who signed the treaty, a dress distinguishing him as Chief.
• For braves and for councillors of each Chief a dress; it being supposed that the braves and councillors will be two for each Chief.
• For each Chief, except Yellow Quill, a buggy.
• For the braves and councillors of each Chief, except Yellow Quill, a buggy.
• In lieu of a yoke of oxen for each reserve, a bull for each, and a cow for each Chief; a boar for each reserve and a sow for each Chief, and a male and female of each kind of animal raised by farmers, these when the Indians are prepared to receive them.
• A plough and a harrow for each settler cultivating the ground.
• These animals and their issue to be Government property, but to be allowed for the use of the Indians, under the superintendence and control of the Indian Commissioner.
• The buggies to be the property of the Indians to whom they are given.
• The above contains an inventory of the terms concluded with the Indians.

WEMYSS M. SIMPSON,
MOLYNEUX St. JOHN,
A. G. ARCHIBALD,
JAS. McKAY.

Endnotes

Notes to Introduction

1   Manitoba Indian Brotherhood, *Wahbung: Our Tomorrows* (Winnipeg: Manitoba Indian Brotherhood, 1971) at viii.

2   I use the term "Indigenous" broadly to refer to the many Indigenous nations of first peoples of Canada. The term "Aboriginal" is used in the context of "Aboriginal peoples of Canada" as defined in the *Constitution Act, 1982*, being Schedule B to the *Canada Act, 1982* (U.K.), 1982, c. 11. At times, I use the term "Indian" to reflect the use of the term by certain authors or in certain circumstances, especially historical. At other times I will refer in particular to the Anishinabe people or nation, a term which I define at page 123, note 19.

3   Charlie Nelson, personal communication (21 July 2011).

4   James Sa'ke'j Youngblood Henderson argues that "[t]he shared meaning of a specific Treaty relation can be found in understanding and interpreting the wording of a Treaty text from each language. Each category in the Treaty text is embedded with competing historical and legal context as well as the shared intent and purposes of the Treaty parties. This makes finding a clear understanding of the Treaty text challenging." James (Sa'ke'j) Youngblood Henderson, *Treaty Rights in the Constitution of Canada* (Toronto: Thomson Canada, 2007) at 34 [Henderson, *Treaty Rights*].

5   Peter Atkinson, RCAP submissions, December 8, 1992, Roseau River First Nation, at 207.

6   Support for this work is found in Arthur Ray, Jim Miller, & Frank Tough, *Bounty and Benevolence: A History of Saskatchewan Treaties* (Montreal and Kingston: McGill-Queen's University Press, 2000) at 69 [Ray, Miller & Tough]: "Treaty-making involved an unequal meeting of two property systems. Unfortunately, this aspect of the process has not received much attention, and it is poorly understood, in part because the terms describing ownership, land use, and occupancy are used in an imprecise way in the historical records and scholarly literature. Furthermore, conflicting scholarly theories about the nature of Aboriginal tenure systems add to the confusion." It is also found in John Borrows, *Canada's Indigenous Constitution* (Toronto: University of Toronto Press, 2010) at 20 [Borrows, *Indigenous Constitution*].

7   *R. v. Sundown*, [1999] 1 S.C.R. 393 at para. 24; see also *R. v. Badger*, [1996] 1 S.C.R. 771 at para. 76. [Badger]

8   *Badger*, *ibid.* at para 52; cited with approval in *Mikisew Cree First Nation* v. *Canada (Minister of Canadian Heritage)*, [2005] 3 S.C.R. 388 at para. 29.

9   *R. v. Taylor and Williams*, [1981] 3 C.N.L.R. 114 (Ont. C.A.) at 236: cited with approval in *Delgamuukw* v. *British Columbia*, [1997] 3 S.C.R. 1010 at para. 87 and *R. v. Sioui*, [1990] 1 S.C.R. 1025 at 1045.

10 According to Dickson C.J.C. for the court in *Mitchell* v. *Peguis Indian Band*, [1990] 2 S.C.R. 85 at para. 15, "The *Nowegijick* principles must be understood in the context of this Court's sensitivity to the historical and continuing status of aboriginal peoples

in Canadian society. . . . It is Canadian society at large which bears the historical burden of the current situation of native peoples and, as a result, the liberal interpretive approach applies to any statute relating to Indians, even if the relationship thereby affected is a private one. Underlying *Nowegijick* is an appreciation of societal responsibility and a concern with remedying disadvantage, if only in the somewhat marginal context of treaty and statutory interpretation."

11 See, e.g., Leonard R. Rotman, "Taking Aim at the Canons of Treaty Interpretation in Canadian Aboriginal Rights Jurisprudence" (1997) 46 U.N.B.L.J. 11.

12 Wilson J., dissenting (Dickson C.J.C. and L'Heureux-Dubé J. concurring) in *R. v. Horseman*, [1990] 1 S.C.R. 901.

13 *Constitution Act, 1982, supra* note 2.

14 See, e.g., the work of Michael Asch, Sa'ke'j Henderson, Patrick Macklem, Kent McNeil, Patricia Monture, Brian Slattery, Mark Walters, etc.

15 As John Borrows states: "[T]here are problems with theories of discovery, occupation, prescription, and conquest when considering the place of Indigenous legal traditions in Canada's legal hierarchy. Fortunately, there is an alternative. We do not have to abandon *law* to overcome past injustices. . . . we only have to relinquish those *interpretations of law* that are discriminatory. Working out the fuller implications of treaties between Indigenous peoples and the Crown is a way out of the impasse created by the rejection of other legal theories. Treaties have the potential to build Canada on more solid ground." Borrows, *Indigenous Constitution, supra* note 6 at 20.

16 Sidney L. Harring, *White Man's Law: Native People in Nineteenth-Century Canadian Jurisprudence* (Toronto: University of Toronto Press, 1998) at 241.

17 See, in particular, John Borrows, *Recovering Canada: The Resurgence of Indigenous Law* (Toronto: University of Toronto Press, 2002), and Borrows, *Indigenous Constitution, supra* note 6.

18 See, e.g., John Borrows, "Wampum at Niagara: The Royal Proclamation, Canadian Legal History, and Self-Government" in Michael Asch (Ed.), *Aboriginal and Treaty Rights in Canada* (Vancouver: UBC Press, 1997) 155 [Borrows, "Wampum at Niagara"]; Sharon Venne, "Understanding Treaty 6: An Indigenous Perspective" in Asch, *ibid.*, at 173.

19 Robert A. Williams Jr., *Linking Arms Together: American Indian Treaty Visions of Law & Peace*, 1600–1800 (New York: Oxford University Press, 1997) at 12 [Williams].

20 See also Office of the Treaty Commissioner, *Treaty Implementation: Fulfilling the Covenant* (Saskatoon: Office of the Treaty Commissioner, 2007) at 5: "The treaties with the Crown are sacred covenants, made among three parties — the First Nations and an undivided Crown, as sovereign nations, and the Creator. In their view, a permanent relationship of mutual respect and sharing was thus established. The unwavering conviction of the Treaty First Nations is that the treaties include not only the written texts recorded by the Crown and the oral agreements made at the time of each treaty, but also their very spirit and intent, and that the treaties govern every aspect of their relationship with the Crown, and, through the Crown, with all non-First Nations

peoples. In this view, the treaties are holistic in their relevance to all dealings between the Parties and have political, legal and sacred status. It is through these agreements with the Crown that the First Nations gave their consent to sharing their territories with newcomers from overseas and their descendants, and that a unique and eternal relationship between the First Nations and the Crown was forged."

21   Harold Johnson, *Two Families: Treaties and Government* (Saskatoon: Purich, 2007) at 29.

22   Heidi Kiiwetinepinesiik Stark, "Respect, Responsibility and Renewal: The Foundations of Anishinaabe Treaty Making with the United States and Canada" (2010) 34 *American Indian Culture and Research J.* 145 at 156.

23   John Borrows, *Drawing Out Law: A Spirit's Guide* (Toronto: University of Toronto Press, 2010) at 8.

24   See Craft, "Living Treaties, Breathing Research," *Canadian Journal of Women and the Law* [forthcoming].

25   Treaty No. 1, 1871 (Ottawa: Edmond Cloutier, Queen's Printer and Controller of Stationery, 1957).

Notes to Chapter 1

1   Jean Friesen, "Grant Me Wherewith to Make My Living," in Kerry Abel & Jean Friesen (Eds.), *Aboriginal Resource Use in Canada* (Winnipeg, University of Manitoba Press, 1991) 141 [J. Friesen, "To Make My Living"]; Jean Friesen, "Magnificent Gifts: The Treaties of Canada with Indians of the Northwest, 1869–76" (1986) 5:1 *Transactions of the Royal Society of Canada* 41 [J. Friesen, "Magnificent Gifts"].

2   J. R. Miller, *Compact, Contract, Covenant: Aboriginal Treaty-Making in Canada* (Toronto: University of Toronto Press, 2009) [Miller].

3   J. Friesen, "Magnificent Gifts," *supra* note 1.

4   G. F. G. Stanley, *The Birth of Western Canada: A History of the Riel Rebellions* (Toronto: University of Toronto Press, 1936) at 213.

5   D. J. Hall, "'A Serene Atmosphere?' Treaty One Revisited" (1984) 4 *Canadian J. of Native Studies* 321 at 332.

6   *Ibid.* at 322.

7   *Ibid.* at 328.

8   J. Friesen, "To Make My Living," *supra* note 1.

9   J. Friesen, "Magnificent Gifts," *supra* note 1 at 43.

10   *Ibid.* at 49.

11   Kinship fostered reciprocal obligations and alliances and allowed for exchange. According to Friesen, at the treaty negotiations, "The commissioners are called Brothers who represent the queen, but who are nevertheless in the same position relative to Her Majesty as the Indian 'children'. . . . In the fur-trade alliances the factor had been ad-

dressed as father, for he served in one sense as provider and supplier. Similarly, to take the hand of the Great White Mother indicated that one accepted that the Queen would 'clothe' the Indians — that is, that protection and material wants were part of what was being offered whether or not it was written in such precise terms. In using such language the treaty commissioners were accepting an implied moral responsibility of greater proportions than they realized." *Ibid.* at 47.

12   *Ibid.* at 48–49.

13   Bruce M. White, "'Give Us a Little Milk': The Social and Cultural Meanings of Gift Giving in the Lake Superior Fur Trade" (1982) 48 *Minnesota History* 60 at 62.

14   Arthur Ray, Jim Miller & Frank Tough, *Bounty and Benevolence: A History of Saskatchewan Treaties*, (Montreal and Kingston: McGill-Queen's University Press, 2000) at 63 [Ray, Miller & Tough].

15   Sidney L. Harring, *White Man's Law: Native People in Nineteenth-Century Canadian Jurisprudence* (Toronto: University of Toronto Press, 1998) at 251.

16   Ray, Miller & Tough, *supra* note 14 at 86.

17   See Janna Promislow, "One Chief, Two Chiefs, Red Chiefs, Blue Chiefs: Newcomer Perspectives on Indigenous Leadership in Rupert's Land and the North-West Territories," in Hamar Foster, Benjamin L. Berger & A. R. Buck (Eds.), *The Grand Experiment: Law and Legal Culture in British Settler Societies* (Vancouver: UBC Press, 2009) in which the author moves beyond the treaty record into the relationships that precede and shape the treaty. In particular, Promislow looks to the HBC trading practices and their relationships with the Indigenous trading partners (including kinship and ceremonial elements, similar to Jean Friesen's work) to illustrate the symbolic acts of recognition that overlapped the fur trade and the treaty negotiations.

18   "Turtle Island" is the term used by the Anishinabe and other Indigenous peoples to describe what is geo-politically known as North America. This terminology relates to creation stories in which the turtle is generally described as having emerged from the great flood to carry on her back a new home for the Indigenous peoples.

19   In this context, I refer broadly to the Anishinabe nation (encompassing all of the Anishinabe sub-groups) and use the term "groups" (or "tribes") to identify the smaller groups or independent collectivities within that broader structure, many of which were identified as decision-making authorities in the process of treaty making.

20   Leanne Simpson, "Looking after Gdoo-naaganinaa: Precolonial Nishnaabeg Diplomatic and Treaty Relationships" (2008) 23 *Wicazo Sa Rev.* 29 at 32 [Simpson, "Looking after Gdoo-naaganinaa"] at 29.

21   Also referred to as the "Ojibway Confederacy" or "Western Lake Confederacy."

22   Peter Jones, *History of the Ojebway Indians with Especial Reference to Their Conversion to Christianity* (London: A. W. Bennet, 1861) at 39.

23   Simpson, "Looking after Gdoo-naaganinaa," *supra* note 20 at 39.

24   Robert A. Williams Jr., *Linking Arms Together: American Indian Treaty Visions of Law & Peace, 1600–1800* (New York: Oxford University Press, 1997) at 33 [Williams] .

25   *Ibid.* at 36.

26   Ipperwash Inquiry, *Crown and Aboriginal Occupations of Land: A History and Comparison*, by John Borrows (Ontario: Ministry of the Attorney General, 2005) at 5 [Borrows, *Occupations of Land*].

27   See Heidi Bohaker, "Anishinaabe Toodaims: Contexts for Politics, Kinship and Identity in the Eastern Great Lakes" in Carolyn Podruchny & Laura Peers (Eds.), *Gathering Places: Aboriginal and Fur Trade Histories* (Vancouver: UBC Press, 2010) [Peers, *Fur Trade Histories*].

28   See Victor P. Lytwyn, "A Dish with One Spoon: The Shared Hunting Grounds Agreement in the Great Lakes and St. Lawrence Valley Region," in David H. Pentland (Ed.), *Papers of the 28th Algonquian Conference* (Winnipeg, Manitoba: University of Manitoba, 1997) at 210.

29   Simpson, "Looking after Gdoo-naaganinaa," *supra* note 20.

30   Williams, *supra* note 24 at 126.

31   John Tanner, Edwin James & Charles Daudert, *The Narrative of John Tanner "The Falcon": His Captivity — His Thirty Years with the Indians* (1830; reprinted Kalamazoo: Hansa-Hewlett, 2009).

32   *The Nor'Wester* (14 March 1860).

33   Williams, *supra* note 24 at 62.

34   *Ibid.* at 50.

35   *Ibid.* at 32.

36   John S. Long, *Treaty No. 9: Making the Agreement to Share the Land in Far Northern Ontario in 1905* (Montreal & Kingston: McGill-Queen's University Press, 2010) at 19. [Long, *Treaty No. 9*].

37   See Sylvia Van Kirk, *Many Tender Ties: Women in Fur-Trade Society in Western Canada 1670–1870* (Winnipeg: Watson & Dwyer, 1980) [Van Kirk], and Jennifer S. H. Brown, *Strangers in Blood: Fur Trade Company Families in Indian Country* (Norman: University of Oklahoma Press, 1980).

38   *Connolly* v. *Woolrich* (1867), 17 R.J.R.Q. 75 (Q.S.C.).

39   Arthur J. Ray, *Indians in the Fur Trade: Their Role as Trappers, Hunters, and Middlemen in the Lands Southwest of Hudson Bay, 1660–1870* (Toronto: University of Toronto Press, 1974); Arthur J. Ray & Donald B. Freedman, *Give Us Good Measure: An Economic Analysis of Relations between the Indians and the Hudson's Bay Company before 1763* (Toronto: University of Toronto Press, 1978).

40   Richard White, *The Middle Ground: Indians, Empires and Republics in the Great Lakes Region, 1650–1815* (Cambridge: Cambridge University Press, 1991) [R. White, *Middle Ground*].

41   *Ibid.*

42   *Ibid.* at x.

43   *Ibid.* at 52.

44   Janna Promislow, "'Thou Wilt Not Die of Hunger . . . For I Bring Thee Merchandise':
      Consent, Intersocietal Normativity, and the Exchange of Food at York Factory, 1682-
      1763," in Jeremy Webber & Colin M. Macleod (Eds.), *Between Consenting Peoples: Pol-
      itical Community and the Meaning of Consent* (Vancouver: UBC Press, 2010) 77 at 82
      [Promislow, "Merchandise"].

45   "The Royal Charter for Incorporating the Hudson's Bay Company, A.D. 1670," online:
      www.solon.org/Constitutions/Canada/English/PreConfederation/hbc_charter_1670.
      html.

46   Note that southern Manitoba and the area of Treaty One are within the Hudson's Bay
      drainage basin.

47   *The Royal Proclamation of 1763*, reprinted in R.S.C. 1985, App. II, No. 1, online: www.
      bloorstreet.com/200block/rp1763.htm.

48   *The Canada Jurisdiction Act,* 43 Geo. III, c. 138.

49   See A. S. Morton, "The Canada Jurisdiction Act (1803) and the North-West" (1938) 2
      Transactions of the Royal Society of Canada 121.

50   Borrows, *Occupations of Land, supra* note 26 at 12.

51   *Ibid.* at 11–12.

52   Williams, *supra* note 24 at 21.

53   Gerald Friesen, with A. C. Hamilton & C. M. Sinclair, "'Justice Systems' and Manitoba's
      Aboriginal People: An Historical Survey," in Gerald Friesen (Ed.), *River Road: Essays
      on Manitoba and Prairie History* (Winnipeg: University of Manitoba Press, 1996) at 53
      [G. Friesen, "Justice Systems"].

54   Miller, *supra* note 2 at 12.

55   Promislow, "Merchandise," *supra* note 44 at 87.

56   Williams, *supra* note 24 at 76.

57   For a discussion of Aboriginal women's role in the fur trade, see Van Kirk, *supra note 37.*

58   See Laura Peers & Jennifer Brown, "'There is No End to Relationship among the In-
      dians': Ojibwa Families and Kinship in Historical Perspective" (2000) 4 *History of the
      Family* 529.

59   Miller, *supra* note 2 at 21.

60   See generally Miller, *ibid.*

61   Ray, Miller, and Tough are three prominent researchers and scholarly writers who
      focus on treaties and western Canadian–Aboriginal history. *Bounty and Benevolence* is
      considered to be one of the key written resources relating to the interpretation of the
      numbered treaties.

62   Long, *Treaty No. 9, supra* note 36 at 21.

63 Cory Willmott & Kevin Brownlee, "Dressing for the Homeward Journey: Western Anishinaabe Leadership Roles Viewed through Two Nineteenth-Century Burials" in Peers, *Fur Trade Histories, supra* note 27.

64 Alexander Morris, *The Treaties of Canada with the Indians of Manitoba and the North-West Territories* (1880; reprint, Saskatoon: Fifth House, 1991) at 21 [Morris].

65 *Ibid.* at 285.

66 *Ibid.* at 4.

67 I use the term "Anishinabek" to reflect the plural form and the dialect of the region.

68 R. White, *Middle Ground, supra* note 40.

69 John Borrows, "Wampum at Niagara: The Royal Proclamation, Canadian Legal History, and Self-Government" in Michael Asch (Ed.), *Aboriginal and Treaty Rights in Canada* (Vancouver: UBC Press, 1997) 155 [Borrows, "Wampum at Niagara"].

70 *Ibid.* at 157.

71 Williams, *supra* note 24 at 23.

72 The "Indian Country" included the Anishinabe territory in what would become the Treaty One area.

73 Borrows, "Wampum at Niagara," *supra* note 69 at 160.

74 James (Sa'ke'j) Youngblood Henderson, *Treaty Rights in the Constitution of Canada* (Toronto: Thomson Canada, 2007) at 225 [Henderson, *Treaty Rights*].

75 I have seen a replica of the Covenant Chain Belt and was fortunate to have heard a part of the oral history of the belt being shared at a community-led conference: Inclusion and Representation in Anishinabek Self-Government, Nipissing First Nation, 21-22 January 2011.

76 Borrows, "Wampum at Niagara," *supra* note 69 at 165.

77 Henderson uses the term "Ojibway Confederacy." I prefer to speak of the Anishinabe Nation as the collective group of Anishinabe peoples that exist independently but collectively as Anishinabe people. Henderson, *Treaty Rights, supra* note 74 at 34.

78 *Ibid.* at 226.

79 *Ibid.* at 227.

80 Borrows, "Wampum at Niagara," *supra* note 69 at 169.

81 Mark D. Walters, "'Your Sovereign and Our Father': The Imperial Crown and the Idea of Legal-Ethnohistory" in Shaunnagh Dorsett & Ian Hunters (Eds.), *Law and Politics in British Colonial Thought: Transpositions of Empire* (New York: Palgrave MacMillan, 2010) 91 at 92.

82 Borrows, "Wampum at Niagara," *supra* note 68 at 166.

83 Williams, *supra* note 24 at 11.

84   Miller, *supra* note 2 at 121.

85   See Jill St. Germain, *Indian Treaty-making Policy in the United States and Canada, 1867–1877* (Toronto: University of Toronto Press, 2001), and Francis Paul Prucha, *American Indian Treaties: The History of a Political Anomaly* (Berkeley: University of California Press, 1997).

86   Heidi Kiiwetinepinesiik Stark, "Respect, Responsibility and Renewal: The Foundations of Anishinaabe Treaty Making with the United States and Canada" (2010) 34 *American Indian Culture and Research J.* 145 at 155.

87   I use the term "inter-nation" rather than "international" to avoid the connotations associated with international law.

88   Williams, *supra* note 24 at 9.

89   Henderson, *Treaty Rights, supra* note 74 at 479.

90   G. Friesen, "Justice Systems," *supra* note 53.

91   Long, *Treaty No. 9, supra* note 36 at 22.

Notes to Chapter 2

1   I use the term "band(s)" to refer to the small groups of Anishinabe that generally lived and hunted together and were represented by a common leader in the Treaty One negotiations. They are referred to in the negotiation record as "campfire," meaning those who had camped around the tent of a particular leader and who followed that leader or family head.

2   J. R. Miller, *Compact, Contract, Covenant: Aboriginal Treaty-Making in Canada* (Toronto: University of Toronto Press, 2009) at 163 [Miller].

3   Lord Selkirk to Commissioner S. B. Coltman (17 July 1817), Fort Douglas, Selkirk Papers (C.4.v.II 3809).

4   *Ibid.*

5   *The Nor'Wester* (14 February 1869): an extract from an address of Chief Peguis to the Great House Across the Water.

6   Miller, *supra* note 2 at 150.

7   The area of Treaty One is roughly the equivalent of the Province of Manitoba and the adjoining timber grounds.

8   Gerald Friesen, with A. C. Hamilton & C. M. Sinclair, "'Justice Systems' and Manitoba's Aboriginal People: An Historical Survey," in Gerald Friesen (Ed.), *River Road: Essays on Manitoba and Prairie History* (Winnipeg: University of Manitoba Press, 1996) at 53 [G. Friesen, "Justice Systems"].

9   Assiniboia overlapped significantly with what became the Province of Manitoba in 1870 and the Treaty One territory in 1871.

10   In this case, I am referring to the Red River Métis. For a discussion of the Métis, see Jennifer Brown, "Métis," in *The Canadian Encyclopedia*, online: www.thecanadianen-cyclopedia.com/index.cfm?Params=A1ARTA0005259&PgNm=TCE.

11   *The Manitoba Act*, 1870, 33 Victoria, c. 3, s. 31-32.

12   Robert A. Williams, Jr., *Linking Arms Together: American Indian Treaty Visions of Law & Peace, 1600–1800* (New York: Oxford University Press, 1997) at 23.

13   See Canada, Royal Commission on Aboriginal Peoples, *Perspectives and Realities* (Ottawa: Supply and Services, 1996), c. 5 at 2.1.

14   W. L. Morton, *Manitoba: A History* (Toronto: University of Toronto Press, 1957).

15   G. Friesen, "Justice Systems," *supra* note 8 at 58.

16   *The Manitoba Act*, 1870, *supra* note 11.

17   The articles of Treaty One provide that the parties would be called to "deliberate upon certain matters of interest to Her Most Gracious Majesty, of the one part, and to the said Indians of the other." (Treaty One, 1871, in Alexander Morris, *The Treaties of Canada with the Indians of Manitoba and the North-West Territories* (1880; reprint, Saskatoon: Fifth House, 1991) at 313).

18   James (Sa'ke'j) Youngblood Henderson, *Treaty Rights in the Constitution of Canada* (Toronto: Thomson Canada, 2007) at 228.

19   Report of the Select Committee on the Hudson's Bay Company, 1857.

20   Morris, *supra* note 17 at 9.

21   *Ibid.* at 37.

22   See, e.g., the Selkirk Treaty, negotiated in 1817, which allowed for White settlement of the lots along the Red River, in exchange for an annual rent of 100 pounds of tobacco to each nation. After Lord Selkirk's death, the treaty was not renewed and payments ceased, the land having been sold back to the HBC by Selkirk's successors in 1836.

23   Chief Peguis also noted that, in 1859, fellow Chiefs Makasis, Ke-kisimakirs and Wa-waskasis all sent letters to the Aborigines' Protection Society in London and to Mr. Isbister about the land question in the west. A full account of this was published in *The Nor'Wester* on June 1, 1861.

24   Morris, *supra* note 17 at 25–26.

25   McKay was influential in securing Treaty One and many of the later treaties. "James McKay, a member, at that time, of the Executive council of Manitoba, and himself a half-breed intimately acquainted with the Indian tribes, and possessed of much influence over them." Cited in Morris, *supra* note 17 at 25.

26   Alexander Morris to the Minister of the Interior (18 August 1875), Ottawa, Library and Archives Canada (RG 10, vol. 3624, file 5217-1, C10, 109).

27 See also "Copy of the Indian Agreement" *Nor'Wester*, August 17, 1869. See also Jean Friesen, "I cannot love on promises," report prepared for the Public Interest Law Centre, March 2008.

28 *The Manitoban*, (1871), Winnipeg, Provincial Archives of Manitoba (as transcribed by the Manitoba Treaty and Aboriginal Rights Research Centre, 1970) at 4 [*The Manitoban*].

29 Chief Moosoos to A. Archibald (17 December 1870), Winnipeg, Public Archives of Manitoba (Archibald Papers MG 12, A1).

30 Declaration by the Indians of Portage La Prairie, May 30, 1871, Provincial Archives of Manitoba (emphasis added).

31 *The Manitoban*, *supra* note 28 at 2–3.

32 *Ibid.* at 1.

33 Canada, "Instructions from Canada to the Treaty Commission" in *Sessional Papers*, No. 20 (1870):

1. You will, with as little delay as possible, open communication with the Indian Bands occupying the country lying between Lake Superior and the Province of Manitoba, with a view to the establishment of such friendly relations as may make the route from Thunder Bay to Fort Garry secure at all seasons of the year, and facilitate the settlement of such portion of the country as it may be practicable to improve.

2. You will also turn your attention promptly to the condition of the country outside the Province of Manitoba, on the North and West; and while assuring the Indians of your desire to establish friendly relations with them, you will ascertain and report to His Excellency the course you may think most advisable to pursue, whether by treaty or otherwise, for the removal of any obstructions that may be presented to the flow of population into the fertile lands that lie between Manitoba and the Rocky Mountains.

3. You will also make a full report upon the state of the Indian Tribes now in the Territories; their numbers, wants and claims, the system heretofore pursued by the Hudson's Bay Company in dealing with them, accompanied by any suggestions you may desire to offer with.

34 Morris, *supra* note 17 at 37.

35 *Ibid.* at 27.

36 *Ibid.* at 25.

37 *The Manitoban*, *supra* note 28 at 12.

38 Treaty Three was later made with these same bands by Commissioner Morris in 1873.

39 Morris, *supra* note 17 at 26.

40 *Ibid.* at 32.

41 *Ibid.* at preface.

Notes to Chapter 3

1   Letter from Lieutenant-Governor Archibald to Secretary of State, cited in Alexander Morris, *The Treaties of Canada with the Indians of Manitoba and the North-West Territories* (1880; reprint, Saskatoon: Fifth House, 1991) at 313) at 33 [Morris].

2   *The Manitoba Act*, 1870, 33 Victoria, c. 3, s. 31.

3   In the written text of the treaty, the land is described in this way: Beginning at the international boundary line near its junction with the Lake of the Woods, at a point due north from the centre of Roseau Lake; thence to run due north to the centre of Roseau Lake; thence northward to the centre of White Mouth Lake, otherwise called White Mud Lake; thence by the middle of the lake and the middle of the river issuing therefrom to the mouth thereof in Winnipeg River; thence by the Winnipeg River to its mouth; thence westwardly, including all the islands near the south end of the lake, across the lake to the mouth of Drunken River; thence westwardly to a point on Lake Manitoba half way between Oak Point and the mouth of Swan Creek; thence across Lake Manitoba in a line due west to its western shore; thence in a straight line to the crossing of the rapids on the Assiniboine; thence due south to the international boundary line; and thence eastwardly by the said line to the place of beginning.

4   *The Manitoban* (1871), Winnipeg, Provincial Archives of Manitoba (as transcribed by the Manitoba Treaty and Aboriginal Rights Research Centre, 1970) at 6 [*The Manitoban*].

5   *Ibid.* at 8.

6   Morris, *supra* note 1 at 27.

7   Notes of an interview between the Lieutenant-Governor of Manitoba and Henry Prince, Miskookenew, Chief of the Saulteux and Swampies (13 September 1870), Winnipeg, Public Archives of Manitoba (Archibald Papers, MG 12, A1).

8   Morris, *supra* note 1 at 27.

9   *Ibid.* at 29.

10 *The Manitoban*, *supra* note 4 at 10 (emphasis added).

11 Morris, *supra* note 1 at 31.

12 Morris, *supra* note 1 at 28-29.

13 *Ibid.* at 39.

14 *Ibid.* at 31.

15 *The Manitoban*, *supra* note 4 at 26.

16 *Ibid.*

17 *Ibid.* at 28.

18 *Ibid.* at 29.

19 Morris, *supra* note 1 at 34.

20 *The Manitoban, supra* note 4 at 20–21.

21 *Ibid.* at 28.

22 *Ibid.* at 27.

23 *Ibid.* at 25.

24 Morris, *supra* note 1 at 34.

25 *The Manitoban, supra* note 4 at 31.

26 Letter from Lieutenant-Governor Archibald to Secretary of State, 29 July 1871, cited in Morris, *supra* note 1 at 33.

27 *The Manitoban, supra* note 4 at 20.

28 *Ibid.* at 29.

29 *Ibid.*

30 *Ibid.* at 31.

31 *Ibid.* at 21.

32 *Ibid.* at 30.

33 See, e.g., James Tully, *A Discourse on Property: John Locke and his Adversaries*, 2nd ed. (Cambridge: Cambridge University Press, 1982), and James Tully, *An Approach to Political Philosophy: Locke in Contexts* (Cambridge: Cambridge University Press, 1993).

34 The courts have cautioned against the framing of Aboriginal and treaty rights "on the basis of the philosophical precepts of the liberal enlightenment." *R. v. Van der Peet*, [1996] 2 S.C.R. 507 at para 19.

35 *The Manitoban, supra* note 4 at 31.

36 *Ibid.* at 30–31.

37 *Ibid.* at 31.

38 *Ibid.*

39 *Ibid.*

40 *Ibid.* at 32.

41 *Ibid.* at 33.

42 *Ibid.*

43 *Ibid.* at 35.

44 *Ibid.*

45 *Ibid.* at 37.

46 *Ibid.*

47 *Ibid.*

48 *Ibid.* at 37–38.

49 In the Anishinabe culture, humour is often used to diffuse tense situations. It is most probable that the Anishinabe were laughing at the idea of the commissioner becoming Anishinabe.

50 *The Manitoban, supra* note 4 at 38.

51 *Ibid.*

52 *Ibid.* at 39.

53 Indian Tribes of Manitoba, Manitoba Indian Brotherhood, *Wahbung: Our Tomorrows* (Winnipeg: Manitoba Indian Brotherhood, 1971).

54 Jean Friesen, "Magnificent Gifts: The Treaties of Canada with Indians of the Northwest, 1869-76" (1986) 5:1 *Transactions of the Royal Society of Canada* 41 at 141.

55 Doris Pratt, Harry Bone, & the Treaty and Dakota Elders of Manitoba, with contributions by the Assembly of Manitoba Chiefs Council of Elders & Darren H. Courchene, *Untuwe Pi Kin He — Who We Are: Treaty Elders' Teachings,* Vol. 1 (Winnipeg: Treaty Relations Commission of Manitoba and Assembly of Manitoba Chiefs, 2011) at 28 [Pratt].

56 Victor Courchene, "Treaty 1," DVD: *Elders Treaty Video Series* (Winnipeg: The Manitoba First Nations Education Resource Centre, 2005) [V. Courchene].

57 Charlie Nelson, RCAP submissions, December 8, 1992, Roseau River First Nation, at 213.

58 *The Manitoban, supra* note 4 at 13.

59 *Ibid.* at 21–22.

60 Jennifer S. H. Brown & Susan Elaine Grey (Eds.), *A. Irving Hallowell — Contributions to Ojibwe Studies: Essays, 1934–1972* (Lincoln: University of Nebraska Press, 2010) at 145 [Hallowell, *Essays*].

61 *Ibid.* at 112.

62 Pratt, *supra* note 55 at 77.

63 Hallowell, *Essays, supra* note 60 at 271.

64 V. Courchene, *supra* note 56.

65 Canada, Royal Commission on Aboriginal Peoples, Vol. 1. (Ottawa: Supply and Services, 1996)

Notes to Chapter 4

1 I note that from a western worldview, stone might be considered as cold, rigid, and immovable; from an Anishinabe perspective stone is considered to be an animate object with which we are in relation. It has been shared with me that the stones that formed part of the wall of the Stone Fort are considered to be "witnesses" to the making of Treaty One.

2   Sally Engle Merry, "Legal Pluralism" (1988) 22 *Law & Soc'y Rev.* 869 at 878.

3   Gordon R. Woodman, "Ideological Combat and Social Observation: Recent Debate about Legal Pluralism" (1998) 42 *J. Legal Pluralism* 21.

4   Lon L. Fuller, "Human Interaction and the Law" (1969) 14 *Am J. Juris.* 1 at 1.

5   Jeremy Webber, "The Grammar of Customary Law" (2009) 54 *McGill L.J.* 579 at 581.

6   *Ibid.* Webber convincingly argues that law is culturally shaped and suggests that the language used to conceptualize and analyze the normative content is itself infused with normative content. Webber's reflection is particularly important in the context of Indigenous legal systems, given that context and normativity are infused into the language we use to understand law.

7   John Borrows, *Canada's Indigenous Constitution* (Toronto: University of Toronto Press, 2010) at 7 [Borrows, *Indigenous Constitution*].

8   *Ibid.* at 12.

9   See Borrows generally and, particularly, Borrows, *ibid.* at 16.

10   *Haida Nation* v. *British Columbia (Minister of Forests)*, [2004] 3 S.C.R. 511, at para. 25.

11   See Brian Slattery, "Making Sense of Aboriginal and Treaty Rights" (2000) 79 *Can. Bar Rev.* 196.

12   See James (Sa'ke'j) Youngblood Henderson, "Empowering Treaty Federalism" (1994) 58 *Sask. L. Rev.* 329.

13   Borrows, *Indigenous Constitution, supra* note 7 at 21.

14   See, e.g., Val Napoleon & Hadley Friedland, "An Inside Job: Developing Scholarship from an Internal Perspective of Indigenous Legal Traditions" (Paper provided to Thinking About and Practising with Indigenous Legal Traditions: An Exploratory Workshop, Fort St. John, BC, 30 September–2 October 2011) [unpublished].

15   Roughly the area of the Province of Manitoba (as it was in 1871, the "postage stamp province") plus the timber lands to the north and east.

16   See Jeremy Webber, "Relations of Force and Relations of Justice: The Emergence of Normative Community between Colonists and Aboriginal Peoples" (1995) 33:4 *Osgoode Hall L.J.* 623 [Webber, "Relations of Force"]. See also Mark D. Walters, "Histories of Colonialism Legality and Aboriginality" (2007) 57 U.T.L.J. 819.

17   For a discussion on intersocietal normativity in the context of the fur trade, see Janna Promislow, "'Thou Wilt Not Die of Hunger . . . For I Bring Thee Merchandise': Consent, Intersocietal Normativity, and the Exchange of Food at York Factory, 1682–1763," in Jeremy Webber & Colin M. Macleod (Eds.), *Between Consenting Peoples: Political Community and the Meaning of Consent* (Vancouver: UBC Press, 2010) 77 at 82 [Promislow, "Merchandise"].

18   Webber, "Relations of Force," *supra* note 16 at 626.

19   Particularly the Hudson's Bay Company but to some extent the North West Company as well.

20   See, generally, J. R. Miller, *Compact, Contract, Covenant: Aboriginal Treaty-Making in Canada* (Toronto: University of Toronto Press, 2009) [Miller]; Janna Promislow, "One Chief, Two Chiefs, Red Chiefs, Blue Chiefs: Newcomer Perspectives on Indigenous Leadership in Rupert's Land and The North-West Territories," in Hamar Foster, Benjamin L. Berger & A. R. Buck (Eds.), *The Grand Experiment: Law and Legal Culture in British Settler Societies* (Vancouver: UBC Press, 2009) [Promislow, "One Chief"]; Jean Friesen, "Grant Me Wherewith to Make My Living" in Kerry Abel & Jean Friesen (Eds.), *Aboriginal Resource Use in Canada* (Winnipeg, University of Manitoba Press, 1991) 141 [J. Friesen, "To Make My Living"]; Jean Friesen, "Magnificent Gifts: The Treaties of Canada with Indians of the Northwest, 1869-76" (1986) 5:1 *Transactions of the Royal Society of Canada* 41 [J. Friesen, "Magnificent Gifts"].

21   Webber, "Relations of Force," *supra* note 16 at 657.

22   I use the term "western state law" as a general term to define systems outside Indigenous legal systems. Note that this "western law" might be variously British, Canadian, or Manitoban. This nuance is important because the Treaty One territory covers roughly the Province of Manitoba (created in 1870) and the timber areas outside of the province (and within Rupert's Land). In 1670, Rupert's Land was granted to the Hudson's Bay Company by the British Crown. It was then sold to Canada in 1870. Following a resistance in Manitoba (1869) protesting the annexation of the Red River area (later Manitoba) to Canada as a "territory," the Province of Manitoba was created (1870). The rest of Rupert's Land was transferred to Canada and remained territories (until some of the areas joined in confederation as provinces).

23   In 1871, western law was generally inapplicable to Indians in the Treaty One area. See, generally, Gerald Friesen, *The Canadian Prairies: A History* (Toronto, University of Toronto Press, 1984); Gerald Friesen, *River Road: Essays on Manitoba and Prairie History* (Winnipeg, University of Manitoba Press, 1996); J. Friesen, "To Make My Living," *supra* note 20; Jean Friesen, "Magnificent Gifts," *supra* note 20; James Morrison, *Treaty One of 1871: Background, Context and Understanding of the Parties* (Winnipeg: Opinion Report for Public Interest Law Centre, 2003); James Morrison, *The Robinson Treaties of 1850: A Case Study* (Ottawa: Royal Commission on Aboriginal Peoples, 1996).

24   John Borrows, *Drawing Out Law: A Spirit's Guide* (Toronto: University of Toronto Press, 2010) at 8 [Borrows, *Drawing Out Law*].

25   Basil Johnston, *Honour Earth Mother: Mino-Audjaudauh Mizzu-Kummik-Quae* (Cape Croker, Ont.: Kegedonce Press, 2003) at vii [B. Johnston, *Honour Earth Mother*].

26   Gerald Friesen, with A.C. Hamilton & C.M. Sinclair, "'Justice Systems' and Manitoba's Aboriginal People: An Historical Survey" in Gerald Friesen (Ed.), *River Road: Essays on Manitoba and Prairie History* (Winnipeg: University of Manitoba Press, 1996) at 45.

27   See also Inquiry, *Respecting and Protecting the Sacred*, by Darlene Johnston (Ontario: Ministry of the Attorney General, 2006).

28   In Anishinabe cosmology, animate beings include things that are not recognized as animate in western science, such as rocks, trees, clouds, etc. See discussion in Jennifer S. H. Brown & Susan Elaine Grey (Eds.), *A. Irving Hallowell — Contributions to Ojibwe Studies: Essays, 1934–1972* (Lincoln: University of Nebraska Press, 2010) at 273 [Hal-

lowell, *Essays*] at 45 and 539, and in Berrens, William, as told to A. Irving Hallowell, edited with Introductions by Jennifer S. H. Brown & Susan Elaine Gray, *Memories Myths and Dreams of an Ojibwe Leader* (Montreal & Kingston: McGill-Queen's University Press 2009) at 90 and 125.

29 See, e.g., the story in John Borrows, *Recovering Canada: The Resurgence of Indigenous Law* (Toronto: University of Toronto Press, 2002) at 16–20.

30 B. Johnston, *Honour Earth Mother, supra* note 25 at 112.

31 *Ibid.* at vii.

32 Doris Pratt, Harry Bone, & the Treaty and Dakota Elders of Manitoba, with contributions by the Assembly of Manitoba Chiefs Council of Elders & Darren H. Courchene, *Untuwe Pi Kin He — Who We Are: Treaty Elders' Teachings*, Vol. 1 (Winnipeg: Treaty Relations Commission of Manitoba and Assembly of Manitoba Chiefs, 2011) at 113 [Pratt].

33 Borrows, *Drawing Out Law, supra* note 24 at 72.

34 Hallowell, *Essays, supra* note 28 at 273.

35 J. Friesen, "Magnificent Gifts," *supra* note 20; J. Friesen, "To Make My Living" *supra* note 20.

36 Hallowell, *Essays, supra* note 28 at 561.

37 Hallowell uses *pimadiziwin* in the same way that I use *mino-bimaadiziwin*.

38 B. Johnston, *Honour Earth Mother, supra* note 25 at 147.

39 The Anishinabe refer to creation as the moment when time began. For a richer understanding of Anishinabe creation stories, see Basil Johnston, *Ojibway Heritage* (Toronto: McClelland & Stewart, 1976); and Edward Benton-Banai, *The Mishomis Book: The Voice of the Ojibway* (Minneapolis: University of Minnesota Press, 2010).

40 Promislow, "One Chief," *supra* note 20 at 100.

41 *The Manitoban* (1871), Winnipeg, Provincial Archives of Manitoba (as transcribed by the Manitoba Treaty and Aboriginal Rights Research Centre, 1970) at 5 [*The Manitoban*].

42 Alexander Morris, *The Treaties of Canada with the Indians of Manitoba and the North-West Territories* (1880; reprint, Saskatoon: Fifth House, 1991) at 313) at 27 [Morris].

43 *Ibid.* at 38.

44 See John Tanner journal (generally).

45 *The Manitoban, supra* note 41 at 23.

46 *Ibid.* at 35.

47 *Ibid.* at 33.

48 *Ibid.* at 21.

49   B. Johnston, *Honour Earth Mother, supra* note 25 at 147.

50   Parliament, *Sessional Papers,* No. 81 (1867-68).

51   *The Manitoban, supra* note 41 at 21.

52   Morris, *supra* note 42 at 30.

53   *The Manitoban, supra* note 41 at 20.

54   *Ibid.* at 19.

55   *Ibid.* at 19-20.

56   *Ibid.* at 19.

57   Morris, *supra* note 42 at 31.

58   Lieutenant-Governor Archibald to Secretary of State, cited in Morris, *ibid.* at 34.

59   Declaration by the Indians of Portage La Prairie, May 30, 1871, Provincial Archives of Manitoba.

60   John S. Long, *Treaty No. 9: Making the Agreement to Share the Land in Far Northern Ontario in 1905* (Montreal & Kingston: McGill-Queen's University Press, 2010) at 340 [Long, *Treaty No. 9*].

61   Bruce M. White, "'Give Us a Little Milk': The Social and Cultural Meanings of Gift Giving in the Lake Superior Fur Trade" (1982) 48 *Minnesota History* 60 at 61.

62   Mark D. Walters, "'Your Sovereign and Our Father': The Imperial Crown and the Idea of Legal-Ethnohistory," in Shaunnagh Dorsett & Ian Hunters (Eds.), *Law and Politics in British Colonial Thought: Transpositions of Empire* (New York: Palgrave MacMillan, 2010) 91 at 94.

63   *The Manitoban, supra* note 41 at 30.

64   *Ibid.* at 26.

65   *Ibid.* at 8.

66   Morris, *supra* note 42 at 32.

67   Sarah Carter, "'Your Great Mother across the Salt Sea': Prairie First Nations, the British Monarchy and the Vice Regal Connection to 1900" (2004-2005) 48 *Manitoba History* 34 [Carter].

68   Note that the medals that were originally presented to the Treaty One and Treaty Two Chiefs did not depict the handshake that is figured prominently in the later numbered treaty medals (including the Treaty One and Two replacement medals). The Treaty One and Treaty Two medals issued in 1871 depicted four allegories representing timbering, mining, fishing, and agriculture. See Collections Canada: www.collectionscanada.gc.ca/05/0529/052920/05292002_e.html.

69   Carter, *supra* note 67 at 2.

70   Miller, *supra* note 20 at 163 and 293; see also Jack Bumstead, *Lord Selkirk: A Life* (Winnipeg: University of Manitoba Press, 2008).

71   Morris, *supra* note 42 at 42.

72   *The Manitoban, supra* note 41 at 8.

73   *Ibid.* at 15.

74   B. Johnston, *Honour Earth Mother, supra* note 25 at 51.

75   *Ibid.* at 13–14.

76   *Ibid.* at 149.

77   Pratt, *supra* note 32 at 111–112.

78   Leanne Simpson, "Looking after Gdoo-naaganinaa: Precolonial Nishnaabeg Diplomatic and Treaty Relationships" (2008) 23 *Wicazo Sa Rev.* 29 at 29.

79   Robert A. Williams Jr., *Linking Arms Together: American Indian Treaty Visions of Law & Peace, 1600–1800* (New York: Oxford University Press, 1997) at 47–48 [Williams].

80   Pratt, *supra* note 32 at 29.

81   Canada, Royal Commission on Aboriginal Peoples. *Report of the Royal Commission on Aboriginal Peoples.* Vol. 1, *Looking Forward Looking Back* (Ottawa: Canada Communication Group, 1996) at 130.

82   Promislow, "Merchandise," *supra* note 17 at 114.

Notes to Chapter 5

1   James (Sa'ke'j) Youngblood Henderson, *Treaty Rights in the Constitution of Canada* (Toronto: Thomson Canada, 2007) at 237.

2   *The Manitoban* (1871), Winnipeg, Provincial Archives of Manitoba (as transcribed by the Manitoba Treaty and Aboriginal Rights Research Centre, 1970) at 30 [*The Manitoban*].

3   Treaty No. 1, 1871 (Ottawa: Edmond Cloutier, Queen's Printer and Controller of Stationery, 1957) [Treaty One, 1871].

4   *The Manitoban, supra* note 2 at 12.

5   *Ibid.* at 14-15.

6   Chief Sheeship (Fort Alexander) quoted in *The Manitoban, supra* note 2 at 16.

7   Treaty One, 1871, *supra* note 3.

8   Alexander Morris, *The Treaties of Canada with the Indians of Manitoba and the North-West Territories* (1880; reprint, Saskatoon: Fifth House, 1991) at 313) at 42 [Morris].

9   A further area for research includes inquiry into how the kinship relationship with the "mother" may have differed from those between the Anishinabe and their "fathers,"

such as the kings and fur traders who had forged earlier kinship relationships with the Anishinabe. It is interesting to note that, after the treaty was made and reserves were being selected, Lieutenant-Governor Morris had some difficulties with the Portage band, who found that they could not rely on their "mother's" promises and threatened to go to the "Grandfather" with their complaints, referring to the U.S. president.

10   Basil Johnston, *Honour Earth Mother: Mino-Audjaudauh Mizzu-Kummik-Quae* (Cape Croker, Ont.: Kegedonce Press, 2003) at vi–vii [B. Johnston, *Honour Earth Mother*].

11   Dave Courchene Jr. (2003), online: http://www.theturtlelodge.org/daveCourchene. html.

12   Research interviews with Mary Lorraine Mandamin (Sagkeeng First Nation, Manitoba, 12 June 2011), Josie Kipling (Sagkeeng First Nation, Manitoba, 12 June 2011), Mary Maytwayashing (Sagkeeng First Nation, Manitoba, 14 June 2011), Darlene Starr Courchene (Sagkeeng First Nation, Manitoba, 14 June 2011), Dave Courchene (Sagkeeng First Nation, 10 July 2011).

13   Doris Pratt, Harry Bone & the Treaty and Dakota Elders of Manitoba, with contributions by the Assembly of Manitoba Chiefs Council of Elders & Darren H. Courchene, *Untuwe Pi Kin He — Who We Are: Treaty Elders' Teachings,* Vol. 1 (Winnipeg: Treaty Relations Commission of Manitoba and Assembly of Manitoba Chiefs, 2011) at 28–29 [Pratt].

14   *The Manitoban, supra* note 2 at 19.

15   B. Johnston, *Honour Earth Mother, supra* note 10 at 47.

16   Interviews with Darlene Starr Courchene (Sagkeeng First Nation, Manitoba, 14 June 2011) and Mary Maytwayashing (Sagkeeng First Nation, Manitoba, 14 June 2011).

17   Leanne Simpson, *Dancing on Our Turtle 's Back: Stories of Nishnaabeg Re-Creation, Resurgence and a New Emergence* (Winnipeg: Arbeiter Ring, 2011) at 132–134.

18   Leanne Simpson, "Looking after Gdoo-naaganinaa: Precolonial Nishnaabeg Diplomatic and Treaty Relationships" (2008) 23 *Wicazo Sa Rev.* 29.

19   J. R. Miller, *Compact, Contract, Covenant: Aboriginal Treaty-Making in Canada* (Toronto: University of Toronto Press, 2009) at 184 [Miller].

20   *The Manitoban, supra* note 2 at 26.

21   Morris, *supra* note 8 at 29.

22   *The Manitoban, supra* note 2 at 10.

23   Morris, *supra* note 8 at 40.

24   Jennifer S. H. Brown & Susan Elaine Grey (Eds.), *A. Irving Hallowell — Contributions to Ojibwe Studies: Essays, 1934–1972* (Lincoln: University of Nebraska Press, 2010) at 451.

25   Pratt, *supra* note 13 at 30.

26   *The Manitoban, supra* note 3 at 20.

27   *Ibid.* at 29.

28   Morris, *supra* note 8 at 32.

29   John Borrows, *Drawing Out Law: A Spirit's Guide* (Toronto: University of Toronto Press, 2010) at 8.

30   In addition, the role played by women in the treaty negotiations may have some significance, although it is difficult to assess this retrospectively, and with the record being very light on this subject. However, this citation from *The Manitoban* report is interesting, although I will not speculate here on its possible implications: "The daughter of a chief, wearing a couple of medals, and in years being decidedly the shady side of fifty, came forward, shook hands with His Excellency and the Commissioner, and retired; but a new idea seized her and she advanced to the front again, and kissed both the great men, amid the hearty laughter and applause of over 1,000 spectators, red and white. The conference then adjourned." *The Manitoban, supra* note 2 at 21.

Notes to Chapter 6

1   *The Manitoban* (1871), Winnipeg, Provincial Archives of Manitoba (as transcribed by the Manitoba Treaty and Aboriginal Rights Research Centre, 1970) at 19 [*The Manitoban*].

2   *Ibid.* at 25.

3   *Ibid.* at 35.

4   *Ibid.* at 15.

5   *Ibid.* at 15–16.

6   Doris Pratt, Harry Bone, & the Treaty and Dakota Elders of Manitoba, with contributions by the Assembly of Manitoba Chiefs Council of Elders & Darren H. Courchene, *Untuwe Pi Kin He — Who We Are: Treaty Elders' Teachings,* Vol. 1 (Winnipeg: Treaty Relations Commission of Manitoba and Assembly of Manitoba Chiefs, 2011) at 28 [Pratt].

7   Basil Johnston, *Honour Earth Mother: Mino-Audjaudauh Mizzu-Kummik-Quae* (Cape Croker, Ont.: Kegedonce Press, 2003) at 149 [B. Johnston, *Honour Earth Mother*].

8   *Ibid.* at vi.

9   *Ibid.* at vii-viii.

10   Pratt, *supra* note 6 at 18.

11   *Ibid.* at 21.

12   Jennifer S. H. Brown & Susan Elaine Grey (Eds.), *A. Irving Hallowell — Contributions to Ojibwe Studies: Essays, 1934–1972* (Lincoln: University of Nebraska Press, 2010) at 31 [Hallowell, *Essays*].

13   See Charles Bishop, *The Northern Ojibwa and the Fur Trade: An Historical and Ecological Study* (Toronto: Holt, Rinehart and Winston Canada, 1974); and Laura Peers, *The Ojibwa of Western Canada: 1780 to 1870* (Winnipeg: The University of Manitoba Press, 1994); Hallowell *Essays, ibid.*

14   B. Johnston, *Honour Earth Mother, supra* note 7 at xi.

15   Pratt, *supra* note 6 at 29.

16   Hallowell, *Essays, supra* note 12 at 150.

17   B. Johnston, *Honour Earth Mother, supra* note 7 at 83 and 147.

18   *Ibid.* at 147.

19   Alexander Morris, *The Treaties of Canada with the Indians of Manitoba and the North-West Territories* (1880; reprint, Saskatoon: Fifth House, 1991 at 313) at 288 [Morris].

20   B. Johnston, *Honour Earth Mother, supra* note 7 at xv.

21   Leroy Little Bear, "Aboriginal Rights and the Canadian 'Grundnorm'" in J. Rick Pointing (Ed.), *Arduous Journey: Canadian Indians and Decolonization* (Toronto: McClelland & Stewart, 1986) at 247.

22   Hallowell, *Essays, supra* note 12 at 451.

23   John Tanner, Edwin James, & Charles Daudert, *The Narrative of John Tanner "The Falcon": His Captivity — His Thirty Years with the Indians* (1830; reprinted Kalamazoo: Hansa-Hewlett, 2009).

24   Henry Letander, personal communication, October 2005.

25   According to Christine Morris (Black), one must relate to "how human beings came to be patterned into a particular tract of land. . . . This is because a People's cosmological creation stories and events define principles, ideals, values and philosophies, which in turn inform the legal regime. Furthermore, a cosmology can be likened to a theory. A theory is a story of how things happen: this is not different from the creation story, as it is a particular group's theory of how things came to be and, more specifically, how to live in a particular place." Christine Morris (Black), *A Dialogical Encounter with an Indigenous Jurisprudence* (Ph.D. Dissertation, Griffith University, Austl., 2007) at 6 [unpublished].

26   Cited in Sarah Carter, "'Your Great Mother across the Salt Sea': Prairie First Nations, the British Monarchy and the Vice Regal Connection to 1900" (2004–2005) 48 *Manitoba History* 34 at 51 in reference to HBC Archives, "Peguis" Search File (B.235/a/3 fos. 28-28d).

27   *The Manitoban, supra* note 1 at 30.

Notes to Chapter 7

1   Parliament, S. J. Dawson in *Sessional Papers*, No. 81 (1867-68), cited in Alexander Morris, *The Treaties of Canada with the Indians of Manitoba and the North-West Territories* (1880; reprint, Saskatoon: Fifth House, 1991) at 313) at 28 [Morris].

2   Sarah Carter, "'Your Great Mother across the Salt Sea': Prairie First Nations, the British Monarchy and the Vice Regal Connection to 1900" (2004–2005) 48 Manitoba History 34 [Carter].

3   *Ibid.*

4   *Ibid.* at 6.

5   Morris, *supra* note 1 at 126.

6   *Ibid.* at 129.

7   *Ibid.* at 40.

8   *Ibid.* at 128.

9   Memorandum of Things outside of the Treaty Which Were Promised at the Treaty at the Lower Fort, signed the 3rd day of August, A.D. 1871 by Simpson, Archibald, St. John and McKay, reprinted in Morris, *supra* note 1 at 126–127.

10   Canada, *House of Commons Debates* (31 March 1873, Sir John A. MacDonald).

11   Morris, *supra* note 1 at 127.

12   Molyneux St. John to William Spragge (24 February 1873). Ottawa, *Library and Archives Canada* (RG10, vol. 3598, file 1447, C10, 104).

13   *Ibid.*

14   Chief William Asham to the Superintendent-General of Indian Affairs (8 May 1892), Ottawa, National Archives of Canada (RG 10, vol. 3692, file 14069, C10, 121).

15   William Pennyfather, Joseph Kent, Peter Kent, Joseph Henderson, Robert Henderson, Chief and Councillors Fort Alexander to the Department of Indian Affairs (December 1890), Ottawa, National Archives of Canada (RG 20, vol. 3788, file 43856, C10, 138).

16   Chief Naskepenais to Department of Indian Affairs (17 June 1893), Ottawa, National Archives of Canada (RG 10, vol. 3755, file 30979-4, C10, 133).

17   Chief Naskepenais, Robert Raven, John Raven, Wiassasing, and Enecoo to the Department of Indian Affairs (15 January 1889), Ottawa, National Archives of Canada (RG 10, vol. 3788, file 43856, C10, 138).

18   Letter from F. Ogletree to E. McColl (28 March 1885), Ottawa, National Archives of Canada (RG 10, vol. 3692, file 14069).

19   Morris, *supra* note 1 at 129.

20   *Ibid.* at 139.

21   This is possibly Chief Wa-kooish who was present at the treaty negotiations on behalf of the Anishinabe of Roseau River.

22   Chief Wa-quse to Lieutenant-Governor Morris (30 September 1874), Ottawa, National Archives of Canada (RG 10, vol. 3598, file 1447, C10, 104).

23   In a case that interpreted Treaty One in 1998, Judge Giesbrecht stated that "[t]he fact that the Government of Canada in 1875 took the position that it was bound only by those matters specifically written in the text of the treaties, does not relieve either the Government or the Indian parties to Treaty 1 of the verbal promises made during the negotiations preceding the signing of the treaty." *R. v. Nelson*, [1998] 2 C.N.L.R. 137 at para. 374.

Notes to Conclusion

1   Peter Atkinson, personal communication, May 25, 2012.

2   Richard White, *The Middle Ground: Indians, Empires and Republics in the Great Lakes Region, 1650–1815* (Cambridge: Cambridge University Press, 1991) [R. White, *Middle Ground*].

3   Brian Slattery, "Making Sense of Aboriginal and Treaty Rights" (2000) 79 *Can. Bar Rev.* 196.

4   Treaty No. 1, 1871 (Ottawa: Edmond Cloutier, Queen's Printer and Controller of Stationery, 1957) [Treaty One, 1871].

5   *R. v. Morris,* [2006] 2 S.C.R. 915 at para. 24, 2006 SCC 59.

6   Note that the unsuccessful attempts in July 1871 at negotiating with the Anishinabe at the North-West Angle did not take place at an HBC fort.

7   Alexander Morris, *The Treaties of Canada with the Indians of Manitoba and the North-West Territories* (1880; reprint, Saskatoon: Fifth House, 1991) at 29 [Morris].

8   Victor Courchene, "Treaty 1", DVD: *Elders Treaty Video Series* (Winnipeg: The Manitoba First Nations Education Resource Centre, 2005) [V. Courchene].

9   *The Manitoban* (1871), Winnipeg, Provincial Archives of Manitoba (as transcribed by the Manitoba Treaty and Aboriginal Rights Research Centre, 1970) at 20 [*The Manitoban*].

10   Treaty One, 1871, *supra* note 4.

11   *The Manitoban, supra* note 9 at 26.

12   John S. Long, *Treaty No. 9: Making the Agreement to Share the Land in Far Northern Ontario in 1905* (Montreal & Kingston: McGill-Queen's University Press, 2010) at 352.

13   Elmer Courchene, personal communication, June 12, 2010.

14   John Borrows, "Negotiating Treaties and Land Claims: The Impact of Diversity within First Nations Property Interests" (1992) 12 *Windsor Y. B. Access. Just.* 179 at 191.

15   Elmer Courchene, "Share the Land"; Treaty Relations Commission of Manitoba: www.trcm.ca/learning.php.

16   RCAP transcripts, Oct. 30, 1992, Sagkeeng First Nation at 81.

17   Doris Pratt, Harry Bone, & the Treaty and Dakota Elders of Manitoba, with contributions by the Assembly of Manitoba Chiefs Council of Elders & Darren H. Courchene, *Untuwe Pi Kin He — Who We Are: Treaty Elders' Teachings,* Vol. 1 (Winnipeg: Treaty Relations Commission of Manitoba and Assembly of Manitoba Chiefs, 2011) at 45–46 [Pratt].

Bibliography

Treaties

Manitoulin Island Treaty, 1862

Robinson Huron Treaty, 1850

Robinson Superior Treaty, 1850

Selkirk Treaty, 1817

Treaty No. 1, 1871 (Ottawa: Edmond Cloutier, Queen's Printer and Controller of Stationery, 1957).

Treaty No. 2, 1871

Treaty No. 3, 1873

Legislation

Royal Proclamation of 1763, reprinted in R.S.C. 1985, App. II, No. 1 online: www.bloor-street.com/200block/rp1763.htm.

The Canada Jurisdiction Act, 43 Geo. III, c. 138.

The Constitution Act, 1982, being Schedule B to *the Canada Act 1982* (U.K.), 1982, c. 11.

The Constitution Act, 1867, 30 & 31 Victoria, c. 3.

The Manitoba Act, 1870, 33 Victoria, c. 3.

Case Law

Connolly v. Woolrich (1867), 17 R.J.Q. 75 (Q.S.C.).

Delgamuukw v. British Columbia, [1997] 3 S.C.R. 1010.

Haida Nation v. British Columbia (Minister of Forests), [2004] 3 S.C.R. 511.

Mikisew Cree First Nation v. Canada (Minister of Canadian Heritage), [2005] 3 S.C.R. 388.

Mitchell v. Peguis Indian Band, [1990] 2 S.C.R. 85.

R. v. Badger, [1996] 1 S.C.R. 771.

R. v. Horseman, [1990] 1 S.C.R. 901.

R. v. Nelson, [1998] 2 C.N.L.R. 137.

R. v. Sioui, [1990] 1 S.C.R. 1025.

R. v. Sundown, [1999] 1 S.C.R. 393.

R. v. Taylor and Williams, [1981] 3 C.N.L.R. 114 (Ont. C.A.).

R. v. Van der Peet, [1996] 2 S.C.R. 507.

Primary Sources: Government Documents

Canada, Royal Commission on Aboriginal Peoples. *Perspectives and Realities* (Ottawa: Supply and Services, 1996).

Canada, Royal Commission on Aboriginal Peoples. *Report of the Royal Commission on Aboriginal Peoples: Looking Forward Looking Back,* Vol. 1 (Ottawa: Communication Group, 1996).

Canada, *House of Commons Debates* (31 March 1873, Sir John A. MacDonald).

Charlie Nelson, Royal Commission on Aboriginal Peoples submissions, 8 December 1992, Roseau River First Nation.

Elmer Courchene, personal communication, June 12, 2010.

Ipperwash Inquiry, *Crown and Aboriginal Occupations of Land: A History and Comparison*, by John Borrows (Ontario: Ministry of the Attorney General, 2005).

Ipperwash Inquiry, *Respecting and Protecting the Sacred,* by Darlene Johnston (Ontario: Ministry of the Attorney General, 2006).

Manitoba, Legislative Assembly, *Hansard* (12 May 2010) at 3 (Hon. Greg Selinger).

Parliament, S. J. Dawson in *Sessional Papers*, No. 81 (1867-68).

Parliament, "Instructions from Canada to the Treaty Commission" in *Sessional Papers*, No. 20 (1870).

Peter Atkinson, RCAP submissions, 8 December 1992, Roseau River First Nation.

Primary Sources: Archival Documents

Alexander Morris to the Minister of the Interior (18 August 1875), Ottawa, Library and Archives Canada (RG 10, vol. 3624, file 5217-1, C10, 109).

Chief Moosoos to A. Archibald (17 December 1870), Winnipeg, Public Archives of Manitoba (Archibald Papers, MG 12, A1).

Chief Naskepenais to Department of Indian Affairs (17 June 1893), Ottawa, Library and Archives Canada (RG 10, vol. 3755, file 30979-4, CI0, 133).

Chief Naskepenais, Robert Raven, John Raven, Wiassasing, and Enecoo to the Department of Indian Affairs (15 January 1889), Ottawa, Library and Archives Canada (RG 10, vol. 3788, file 43856, C10, 138).

Chief Wa-quse to Lieutenant-Governor Morris (30 September 1874), Ottawa, Library and Archives Canada (RG 10, vol. 3598, file 1447, C10, 104).

Chief William Asham to the Superintendent-General of Indian Affairs (8 May 1892), Ottawa, Library and Archives Canada (RG 10, vol. 3692, file 14069, C10, 121).

F. Ogletree to E. McColl (28 March 1885), Ottawa, Library and Archives Canada (RG 10, vol. 3692, file 14069).

Lord Selkirk to Commissioner S. B. Coltman, Fort Douglas (17 July 1817) Ottawa, Library and Archives Canada (Selkirk Papers, c.4, vol. II, file 3809).

Memorandum of Things outside of the Treaty which Were Promised at the Treaty at the Lower Fort (3 August, 1871) by Simpson, Archibald, St. John and McKay, reprinted in Morris at 126–127.

Molyneux St. John to William Spragge (24 February 1873) Ottawa, Library and Archives Canada (RG10, vol. 3598, file 1447, C10, 104).

Notes of an interview between the Lieutenant-Governor of Manitoba and Henry Prince, Miskookenew, Chief of the Saulteux and Swampies (13 September 1870), Winnipeg, Public Archives of Manitoba (Archibald Papers, MG 12, A1).

William Pennyfather, Joseph Kent, Peter Kent, Joseph Henderson, Robert Henderson, Chief and Councillors of Fort Alexander to the Department of Indian Affairs (December 1890), Ottawa, Library and Archives Canada (RG 20, vol. 3788, file 43856, C10, 138).

Secondary Sources: Monographs, Essays in Collections and Articles

Alfred, Taiaiake. *Peace, Power and Righteousness: An Indigenous Manifesto*, 2nd ed. (Oxford: Oxford University Press, 2009).

_____. *Wasáse: Indigenous Pathways of Action and Freedom* (Toronto: University of Toronto Press, 2009).

Benton-Banai, Edward. *The Mishomis Book: The Voice of the Ojibway* (Minneapolis: University of Minnesota Press 2010).

Berrens, William, as told to A. Irving Hallowell, edited with Introductions by Jennifer S. H. Brown & Susan Elaine Gray. *Memories Myths and Dreams of an Ojibwe Leader* (Montreal & Kingston: McGill-Queen's University Press 2009).

Bishop, Charles. *The Northern Ojibwa and the Fur Trade: An Historical and Ecological Study* (Toronto: Holt, Rinehart & Winston Canada, 1974).

Bohaker, Heidi. "Anishinaabe Toodaims: Contexts for Politics, Kinship and Identity in the Eastern Great Lakes" in Carolyn Podruchny & Laura Peers (Eds.), *Gathering Places: Aboriginal and Fur Trade Histories* (Vancouver: UBC Press, 2010) 93.

Borrows, John. *Canada's Indigenous Constitution* (Toronto: University of Toronto Press, 2010).

_____. *Drawing Out Law: A Spirit's Guide* (Toronto: University of Toronto Press, 2010).

_____. "Negotiating Treaties and Land Claims: The Impact of Diversity within First Nations Property Interests" (1992) 12 *Windsor Y.B. Access. Just.* 179.

_____. *Recovering Canada: The Resurgence of Indigenous Law* (Toronto: University of Toronto Press, 2002).

_____. "Wampum at Niagara: The Royal Proclamation, Canadian Legal History, and Self-Government" in Michael Asch (Ed.), *Aboriginal and Treaty Rights in Canada* (Vancouver: UBC Press, 1997) 155.

Brown, Jennifer S. H. *Strangers in Blood: Fur Trade Company Families in Indian Country* (Norman: University of Oklahoma Press, 1980).

Brown, Jennifer S. H. & Elizabeth Vibert (Eds.) *Reading Beyond Words: Contexts for Native History,* 2nd ed. (Toronto: University of Toronto Press, 2009).

Bumsted, Jack. *Lord Selkirk: A Life* (Winnipeg: University of Manitoba Press, 2008).

Carter, Sarah. "'Your Great Mother across the Salt Sea': Prairie First Nations, the British Monarchy and the Vice Regal Connection to 1900" (2004–2005) 48 *Manitoba History* 34.

Craft, Aimée. *Living Treaties, Breathing Research,* Canadian Journal of Women and the Law [forthcoming].

Densmore, Frances. *Chippewa Customs* (1929; reprint, St. Paul: Minnesota Historical Society, 1979).

Gerald Friesen. *The Canadian Prairies: A History* (Toronto: University of Toronto Press, 1984).

_____. *River Road: Essays on Manitoba and Prairie History* (Winnipeg: University of Manitoba Press, 1996).

Friesen, Gerald, with A. C. Hamilton & C. M. Sinclair, "Justice Systems and Manitoba's Aboriginal People: An Historical Survey" in Gerald Friesen (Ed.), *River Road: Essays on Manitoba and Prairie History* (Winnipeg: University of Manitoba Press, 1996) p. 49.

Friesen, Jean. "Grant Me Wherewith to Make My Living," in Kerry Abel & Jean Friesen (Eds.), *Aboriginal Resource Use in Canada* (Winnipeg, University of Manitoba Press, 1991) 141.

_____. "Magnificent Gifts: The Treaties of Canada with Indians of the Northwest, 1869-76" (1986) 5:1 *Transactions of the Royal Society of Canada* 41.

Fuller, Lon L. "Human Interaction and the Law" (1969) 14 *Am. J. Juris.* 1.

Hall, D. J. "'A Serene Atmosphere?' Treaty One Revisited" (1984) 4:2 *The Canadian J. of Native Studies* 321.

Hallowell, Irving A., edited and with Introductions by Jennifer S. H. Brown & Susan Elaine Gray. *Contributions to Ojibwe Studies: Essays, 1934-1972* (Lincoln: University of Nebraska Press, 2010).

Harring, Sidney L. *White Man's Law: Native People in Nineteenth-Century Canadian Jurisprudence* (Toronto: University of Toronto Press, 1998).

Henderson, James (Sa'ke'j) Youngblood. "Empowering Treaty Federalism" (1994) 58 *Sask. L. Rev.* 329.

_____. *Treaty Rights in the Constitution of Canada* (Toronto: Thomson Canada, 2007).

Indian Tribes of Manitoba. *Wahbung: Our Tomorrows* (Winnipeg: Manitoba Indian Brotherhood, 1971).

Johnson, Harold. *Two Families: Treaties and Government* (Saskatoon: Purich, 2007).

Johnston, Basil. *Honour Earth Mother: Mino-Audjaudauh Mizzu-Kummik-Quae* (Cape Croker, Ont.: Kegedonce Press, 2003).

_____. *Ojibway Heritage* (Toronto: McClelland & Stewart, 1976).

Jones, Peter. *History of the Ojebway Indians with Especial Reference to Their Conversion to Christianity* (London: A. W. Bennet, 1861).

Kohl, Johann Georg. *Kitchi-Gami: Life among the Lake Superior Ojibway* (1860; reprinted St. Paul: Minnesota Historical Society, 1985)

Linklater, Irene. "Treaty Reconciliation — Kiiway-Dibamahdiiwin" (Paper presented at the Canadian Bar Association Aboriginal Law Conference, Winnipeg, 28 April 2011) [unpublished].

Little Bear, Leroy. "Aboriginal Rights and the Canadian 'Grundnorm'" in J. Rick Pointing (Ed.), *Arduous Journey: Canadian Indians and Decolonization* (Toronto: McClelland & Stewart, 1986) 243.

Long, John S. *Treaty No. 9: Making the Agreement to Share the Land in Far Northern Ontario in 1905* (Montreal & Kingston: McGill-Queen's University Press, 2010).

Lytwyn, Victor P. "A Dish with One Spoon: The Shared Hunting Grounds Agreement in the Great Lakes and St. Lawrence Valley Region," in David H. Pentland (Ed.), *Papers of the 28th Algonquian Conference* (Winnipeg, Manitoba: University of Manitoba, 1997) 210.

Merry, Sally Engle. "Legal Pluralism" (1988) 22 *Law & Soc'y Rev.* 869.

Miller, J. R. *Compact, Contract, Covenant: Aboriginal Treaty-Making in Canada* (Toronto: University of Toronto Press, 2009).

Morris, Alexander. *The Treaties of Canada with the Indians of Manitoba and the North-West Territories* (1880; reprint, Saskatoon: Fifth House, 1991).

Morris (Black), Christine. *A Dialogical Encounter with an Indigenous Jurisprudence* (unpublished Ph.D. Dissertation, Griffith University, Austl, 2007)

Morrison, James. *The Robinson Treaties of 1850: A Case Study* (Ottawa: Royal Commission on Aboriginal Peoples, 1996).

_____. *Treaty One of 1871: Background, Context and Understanding of the Parties* (Winnipeg: Opinion Report for Public Interest Law Centre, 2003).

Morton, A. S. "The Canada Jurisdiction Act (1803) and the North-West" (1938) 2 *Transactions of the Royal Society of Canada* 121.

Morton, W. L. *Manitoba: A History* (Toronto: University of Toronto Press, 1957).

Napoleon, Val & Hadley Friedland. "An Inside Job: Developing Scholarship from an Internal Perspective of Indigenous Legal Traditions." (Paper provided to Thinking About and Practising with Indigenous Legal Traditions: An Exploratory Workshop, Fort St. John, BC, 30 September – 2 October 2011) [unpublished].

Office of the Treaty Commissioner. *Treaty Implementation: Fulfilling the Covenant* (Saskatoon: Office of the Treaty Commissioner, 2007).

Peers, Laura. *The Ojibwa of Western Canada: 1780 to 1870* (Winnipeg: The University of Manitoba Press, 1994).

Peers, Laura & Jennifer Brown. "'There is No End to Relationship among the Indians': Ojibwa Families and Kinship in Historical Perspective" (2000) 4 *History of the Family* 529.

Pratt, Doris, Harry Bone, & the Treaty and Dakota Elders of Manitoba, with contributions by the Assembly of Manitoba Chiefs Council of Elders & Darren H. Courchene. *Untuwe Pi Kin He — Who We Are: Treaty Elders' Teachings,* Vol. I (Winnipeg: Treaty Relations Commission of Manitoba and Assembly of Manitoba Chiefs, 2011).

Promislow, Janna. "One Chief, Two Chiefs, Red Chiefs, Blue Chiefs: Newcomer Perspectives on Indigenous Leadership in Rupert's Land and The North-West Territories," in Hamar Foster, Benjamin L. Berger & A. R. Buck (Eds.), *The Grand Experiment: Law and Legal Culture in British Settler Societies* (Vancouver: UBC Press, 2009) 55.

_____. "'Thou Wilt Not Die of Hunger . . . For I Bring Thee Merchandise': Consent, Intersocietal Normativity, and the Exchange of Food at York Factory, 1682-1763" in Jeremy Webber & Colin M. Macleod (Eds.), *Between Consenting Peoples: Political Community and the Meaning of Consent* (Vancouver: UBC Press, 2010) 77.

Prucha, Francis Paul. *American Indian Treaties: The History of a Political Anomaly* (Berkley: University of California Press, 1997).

Ray, Arthur J. *Indians in the Fur Trade: Their Role as Trappers, Hunters, and Middlemen in the Lands Southwest of Hudson Bay, 1660–1870* (Toronto: University of Toronto Press, 1974).

Ray, Arthur J. & Donald B. Freedman. *Give Us Good Measure: An Economic Analysis of Relations between the Indians and the Hudson's Bay Company before 1763* (Toronto: University of Toronto Press, 1978).

Ray, Arthur J., Jim Miller, & Frank Tough. *Bounty and Benevolence: A History of Saskatchewan Treaties* (Montreal and Kingston: McGill-Queen's University Press, 2000).

Rotman, Leonard R. "Taking Aim at the Canons of Treaty Interpretation in Canadian Aboriginal Rights Jurisprudence" (1997) 46 U.N.B.L.J. 11.

Simpson, Leanne. *Dancing on Our Turtle's Back: Stories of Nishnaabeg Re-Creation, Resurgence and a New Emergence* (Winnipeg: Arbeiter Ring, 2011).

_____. "Looking after Gdoo-naaganinaa: Precolonial Nishnaabeg Diplomatic and Treaty Relationships"(2008) 23:2 *Wicazo Sa Rev.* 29.

Slattery, Brian. "Making Sense of Aboriginal and Treaty Rights" (2000) 79 *Can. Bar Rev.* 196.

Smith, Linda Tuhiwai. *Decolonizing Methodologies: Research and Indigenous Peoples* (Dunedin, N.Z.: University of Otago Press, 1999).

St. Germain, Jill. *Indian Treaty-making Policy in the United States and Canada, 1867-1877* (Toronto: University of Toronto Press, 2001).

Stanley, G. F. G. *The Birth of Western Canada: A History of the Riel Rebellions* (Toronto: University of Toronto Press, 1936).

Stark, Heidi Kiiwetinepinesiik. "Respect, Responsibility and Renewal: The Foundations of Anishinaabe Treaty Making with the United States and Canada" (2010) 34 *American Indian Culture and Research J.* 145.

Tanner, John, Edwin James & Charles Daudert. *The Narrative of John Tanner "The Falcon": His Captivity — His Thirty Years with the Indians* (1830; reprinted Kalamazoo: Hansa-Hewlett, 2009).

Tully, James. *A Discourse on Property: John Locke and his Adversaries*, 2nd ed. (Cambridge: Cambridge University Press, 1982)

_____. *An Approach to Political Philosophy: Locke in Contexts* (Cambridge: Cambridge University Press, 1993).

Van Kirk, Sylvia. *Many Tender Ties: Women in Fur-Trade Society in Western Canada 1670–1870* (Winnipeg: Watson & Dwyer, 1980).

Venne, Sharon. "Understanding Treaty 6: An Indigenous Perspective" in Michael Asch (Ed.), *Aboriginal and Treaty Rights in Canada* (Vancouver: UBC Press, 1997) 173.

Walters, Mark D. "Histories of Colonialism Legality and Aboriginality" (2007) 57 U.T.L.J. 819.

_____. "'Your Sovereign and Our Father': The Imperial Crown and the Idea of Legal-Ethnohistory" in Shaunnagh Dorsett & Ian Hunters (Eds.), *Law and Politics in British Colonial Thought: Transpositions of Empire* (New York: Palgrave MacMillan, 2010) 91.

Warren, William W. *History of the Ojibway* People, 2nd ed. (1885; reprint, St. Paul: Minnesota Historical Society, 2009).

White, Bruce M. "'Give Us a Little Milk': The Social and Cultural Meanings of Gift Giving in the Lake Superior Fur Trade" (1982) 48:2 *Minnesota History* 60.

White, Richard. *The Middle Ground: Indians, Empires and Republics in the Great Lakes Region, 1650-1815* (Cambridge: Cambridge University Press, 2011).

Williams, Robert A. Jr. *Linking Arms Together: American Indian Treaty Visions of Law & Peace, 1600-1800* (New York: Oxford University Press, 1997).

Willmott, Cory & Kevin Brownlee. "Dressing for the Homeward Journey: Western Anishinaabe Leadership Roles Viewed through Two Nineteenth-Century Burials," in Carolyn Podruchny & Laura Peers (Eds.), *Gathering Places: Aboriginal and Fur Trade Histories* (Vancouver: UBC Press, 2010) 48.

Webber, Jeremy. "Legal Pluralism and Human Agency" (2006) 44 *Osgoode Hall L.J.* 167.

_____. "Relations of Force and Relations of Justice: The Emergence of Normative Community Between Colonists and Aboriginal Peoples" (1995) 33:4 *Osgoode Hall L.J.*, 623.

_____. "The Grammar of Customary Law" (2009) 54 *McGill L.J.* 579.

Woodman, Gordon R. "Ideological Combat and Social Observation: Recent Debate about Legal Pluralism" (1998) 42 J. *Legal Pluralism* 21.

Secondary Sources: Newspapers

The Manitoban, Winnipeg, Provincial Archives of Manitoba, 1871 (as transcribed by the Manitoba Treaty and Aboriginal Rights Research Centre (T.A.R.R.) 1970).

The Nor'Wester (14 March 1860).

The Nor'Wester (1 June 1861).

The Nor'Wester (14 February 1869).

Research Interviews and Personal Communications

Courchene, Darlene Starr (Sagkeeng First Nation, Manitoba, 14 June 2011).

Courchene, Dave (Sagkeeng First Nation, 10 July 2011).

Courchene, Elmer, personal communication (June 12, 2010).

Kipling, Josie (Sagkeeng First Nation, Manitoba, 12 June 2011).

Letander, Henry, personal communication (20 October 2005).

Mandamin, Mary Lorraine (Sagkeeng First Nation, Manitoba, 12 June 2011).

Maytwayashing, Mary (Sagkeeng First Nation, Manitoba, 14 June 2011).

Nelson, Charlie, personal communication (Roseau River Anishinabe First Nation, 21 July 2011).

Electronic Resources

Brown, Jennifer. "Métis" in *The Canadian Encyclopedia*: www.thecanadianencyclopedia.com/index.cfm?Params=A1ARTA0005259&PgNm=TCE.

Collections Canada. "Treaty Medals":www.collectionscanada.gc.ca/05/0529/052920/05292002_e.html, Accessed September 12, 2005.

Courchene, Dave Jr. (2003): The Turtle Lodge: http://www.theturtlelodge.org/daveCourchene.html.

Courchene, Elmer. "Share the Land": Treaty Relations Commission of Manitoba: www.trcm.ca/learning.php.

Dictionary of Canadian Biography Online, s.v. "Sir Adams George Archibald": www.bio-graphi.ca/index-e.html?PHPSESSID=c254v418atebag743r3cvm61k3.

Linklater, D'Arcy. "After Treaty": Treaty Relations Commission of Manitoba: www.trcm.ca/learning.php.

Whitebird, Dennis. "What Is the TRCM?", online: www.trcm.ca/learning.php.

The Royal Charter for incorporating the Hudson's Bay Company, A.D. 1670: Solon: www.solon.org/Constitutions/Canada/English/PreConfederation/hbc_charter_1670.html.

Video Resources

Victor Courchene, "Treaty 1," DVD: *Elders Treaty Video Series* (Winnipeg: The Manitoba First Nations Education Resource Centre, 2005).

Index

and settlers 39

Canada: not referred to in Treaty One written record 86–87, 93

Canada Jurisdiction Act, section 91(24) 28

Children

autonomy of 89–90

in British law 90, 92

commitment to future 86, 90

common law 15, 64–65, 67–68, 108

consent 32, 36, 37–38, 41, 108

Constitution Act, 1867 40 *1982* 15

Council of Three Fires 24

Courchene, Dave Sr. 11

Courchene, Elmer 113, 114

Courchene, Ken 81–82, 89

Courchene, Victor 61–62, 110

courts: and treaties 14–16

Covenant Chain 31–34, 109

Cree 57

ceding title and rights 112

and European concept of law 77

and Selkirk Treaty 37

Swampy 49–50

and trade 26

Crown

understanding of *inaakonigewin* principles 72, 83, 107–09

understanding of treaty as social contract 22, 60, 90

treaty implementation favouring 14–15, 108–09, 113

treaties with 20, 31–34

See also Treaty One

Dakota 24–25

Dawson, Simon 102

Douglas treaties 61

Dufferin, Earl of 104

equality

for all the Queen's "children" 86, 88, 91–93, 112–13

among Indigenous peoples 74, 91–92

Europeans. *See* Anishinabe: relationships with Europeans

feasting: as affirmative protocol 26, 29, 72, 82, 83

with guests 77–79

fictive kinship 22, 70

fishing: right to continue 34, 51, 63–64, 97, 98, 105–06, 111

Aimée Craft, B.A. (L.-Ph.) (University of Manitoba), LL.B. (University of Ottawa), LL.M. (University of Victoria), is an Indigenous lawyer from Manitoba. She recently completed an interdisciplinary Masters in Law and Society at the University of Victoria. Her thesis is entitled *Breathing Life Into the Stone Fort Treaty* and focuses on understanding and interpreting treaties from an *Anishinabe inaakonigewin* (legal) perspective.

In her legal practice at the Public Interest Law Centre, she has worked with many Indigenous peoples on land, resources, consultation, human rights, and governance issues. She is chair of the Aboriginal Law Section of the Canadian Bar Association and was appointed to the Speaker's Bureau of the Treaty Relations Commission of Manitoba. In 2011, she was the recipient of the Indigenous Peoples and Governance Graduate Research Scholarship.

Her *pro bono* work includes participation in the development of Federal Court Practice Guidelines for Aboriginal Law Matters, including Oral History and Elders Evidence. She is a sessional lecturer and research affiliate at the University of Manitoba Faculty of Law, and has lectured at other universities and presented at conferences in the areas of consultation and accommodation, treaties, Indigenous laws, language rights, and Aboriginal and treaty rights. In 2009, she successfully argued on behalf of language rights advocates in the first entirely French hearing at the Manitoba Court of Appeal.

Aimée is proud of her ancestors, their legacy, and the teachings they have gifted to her and others. She is especially thankful for her family — immediate and extended — and for the land she belongs to.